FOCUS ON THE MAGIC

LEADERS OF THE NEW EARTH SHARE HOW THEY CALL IN MAGIC, BEAUTY AND ABUNDANCE DESPITE LIFE'S CIRCUMSTANCES

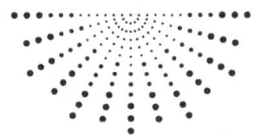

Copyright © 2024 AMA Publishing

All Rights Reserved. Apart from any fair dealing for the purposes of research or private study, or criticism or review, as permitted under the Copyright, Designs and Patents Act 1988, this publication may only be reproduced, stored or transmitted, in any form or by any means, with the prior permission in writing of the copyright owner, or in the case of the reprographic reproduction in accordance with the terms of licensees issued by the Copyright Licensing Agency. Enquiries concerning reproduction outside those terms should be sent to the publisher.

CONTENTS

1. Adriana Monique Alvarez   5
2. Abi Wild Rose   12
3. Alicia Marie Anzaldi   21
4. Amy Danger   31
5. Catherine Cabrera   36
6. Madia Smith   44
7. MBK   52
8. Meg Ashley Korf-Morales   63
9. Rhed Leonard   72
10. Tina Wefer   86
11. Focus on the Magic 22-Day Experience   99

About AMA Publishing   123

1
ADRIANA MONIQUE ALVAREZ

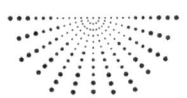

*Y*ou would be shocked by how little control you have in this life.

That was the line that jumped out at me in a podcast interview Derek sent me. This man who had lived in an ashram in India had his Vedic chart read and he couldn't believe how spot-on it all was.

It got me thinking about a moment I had at Groundhog two years ago. Somewhere in a field full of bright yellow flowers I was hit by this awareness that I didn't have nearly as much control as I thought I did.

I had not been interested in believing in destiny or fate because that had always felt like the opposite of freedom and freedom is something I love to feel. But on that summer day, I could feel fate breathing down my neck and I knew I would soon have a new perspective on this topic.

In that two-year period just about everything that could change in my life did. It didn't change because I wanted it to or because I took a new direction. It took a new direction. I remember the point when I realized it was futile to fight it. There wasn't enough will or power in me to do anything about it. Those words shocked me when I felt them and heard them swirling around my head.

How on earth could I believe I create my own reality and believe there was not enough in me to resist what was in motion?

I listened to this podcast and every interview this man ever did, multiple times. I could not let this one go. It felt like it might be part of the puzzle that had been sitting on my table for a while. I was finally at the place where I wasn't confused or angry about the fated events or the new life I had, but I wanted to understand it.

I would wake up with little insights or the capacity to question what had been up until now, set in stone. I could be less emotional when I tested out new theories and I was able to turn it into a game. Thank goodness some humor had returned.

I didn't create this. I would have never chosen this. I didn't ask for this. I didn't want this. Why is it mine?

And then one day, it was right in front of me like a camera lens that finally came into focus...

I didn't choose it two years ago, but I chose it when I came into this reality. Aww. I felt like I had cracked through a wall that led to a new chamber of my being.

When I was pregnant and even when the boys were little people would often tell me they were surprised I wanted to become a mom when freedom and travel are so important to me. The funny thing is, I never saw my kids as a threat to my freedom, but then again I wasn't going to be how moms are expected to be. Both boys were born in the dead of winter and the chances of me sitting at home all day, keeping them wrapped up inside far away from germs and people, wasn't going to happen. I would get everyone dressed and head to coffee shops, malls, and even fine dining from the time they were infants. These boys were going on the ride, and they were amazing.

Kids didn't do it, but living in small-town Colorado was a serious threat to my freedom and the dream life I wanted and had already created. This place is the opposite of freedom. It's roots. It's land, a home, water, ponds, trees, plants, flowers, animals, equipment, trucks, enough food for a hundred years and it weighed on me like a silverback gorilla sitting on my chest. How on earth can I have a big life, living in a small town? I can't. That's what I told myself over and over again until the day I could access a better question…

How can I live a big life in Montezuma County?

At first, nothing came to me. But I sat with it and returned to it daily. I chipped away at my strongly held beliefs, and it started to dribble in.

Do something meaningful that will make someone's day.

How can I get paid for my experience and gifts?

Do what you are good at for someone you care about.

How can I make more money here than I used to?

Blank. Blank. Blank…. cracks, cracks, cracks.

You might be wondering why my most burning questions were about a big life, getting paid, and making more money. It's not only important to me, but also WHO I am. Those are words that will get you dragged through town tied to the back of a horse or get you burned at the stake, right?

I had considered that was part of the package deal with living in the middle of nowhere…living a small life and being poor. I prayed it wasn't, but I considered it might be.

That is until I had my chart read. I thought if I am going to believe in this thing called fate and if this guy is right, that I have so little control over my own life, I at least want to know what freaking life I got. I wanted to see my cards and play the hand as well as I could. And maybe that's just it. That's how free will and fate go hand and hand.

The first thing pointed out in my chart was a triple Scorpio which is precisely why I do deep and think about shit most people could be just fine never thinking. It's why I can't just get high or drunk or join a little spiritual community and check out. It is also why I can't get a government job and be happy with it.

But the thing that gave me the green light and answered my

three burning questions were in my chart, without a doubt, this life, whether I chose it or was assigned it, is to live a big life, be influential, and live well. What a relief!

And there it was right in my chart, a big change at this exact season of my life. A shift from a wild card season of freedom and fun to a time of security and legacy. I didn't know what to feel, but I felt a lot. Within a few days, grief moved in. It had been a bit of a mystery before, but now it felt certain. The old life is over and oh how I wanted to have a funeral and grieve it. One day my mind was racing, and I felt myself darting like a trapped animal who knew there was no getting out alive.

I sat in my truck crying. I just wanted to go to Mexico one more time. I wanted to live without a car one more time. I wanted to hop from AirBNB to AirBNB one more time. I wanted to be in a walkable city one more time. I wanted to eat fifty-cent tacos one more time. I wanted to say goodbye. And none of that was going to happen. It was time to play my cards.

One morning when I walked into the garage to grab a can of tomatoes from the pantry and decided to stay. I looked at the shelves stocked full of food and the buckets full of rice and grains. I had to see it differently. These were not weights around my ankles. They weren't a ball and chain sinking me to the bottom of the ocean. I started going in there to hang out and I went shelf by shelf thinking about each item.

Oh, my favorite balsamic vinegar.

I forgot about these pistachios.

I could use these rose petals in a dessert.

My pantry visits turned into my daily ritual and my heart shifted. I began to feel gratitude wash over me. I could see what I had and how it supported my life and family. The items began to inspire my next meal or party. And at each party, I made sure I expressed how much I appreciated the presence and friendship of those around the table.

I began to float through my days and while I didn't have all the answers to my questions, it didn't seem to matter.

And wouldn't you know on the last day of school, I let the boys sleep in, and I drove them down McElmo Canyon. This place had become my sanctuary and where I receive messages and guidance. On this day I wasn't asking for guidance or thinking about a particular problem or solution. I was daydreaming and noticing the bluest skies and fluffy clouds. There's the final stretch of the canyon where the road straightens out and the view of the LaPlata mountains is ahead. That is where a profound message landed inside of me.

You chose this before you incarnated, and you choose how you feel about it every minute of every day. You create more ease or more chaos with each choice, but there is no changing the path, the lessons, divine timing, and the soul's purpose.

No one wants you to believe in fate or destiny because how on earth can you convince people to work hard if what's to be will be? How could you get them to slave away?

Trusting the path and the mystery could lead to tremendous freedom, ease, and joy. Most people on this planet benefit from the angst humans feel almost non-stop.

If you aren't constantly improving yourself, trying to figure it out, be better, make it happen, and control every possible component, what would you be doing? Enjoying yourself and your life as it is at any given moment?

What about worry, self-doubt, envy, disease, and war? Where can they fit in this kind of human experience?

I felt as if I was no longer sitting on the seat in my truck. There was an awareness that brought a light-as-a-feather feeling that I will never forget. Once again I could appreciate the magic and the mystery that is being a human being.

I am not worried about if this or that will work out as planned or when this will happen. I am not concerned with whether I can trust a person or not. I have no idea how it will unfold. I am not making anything happen. I am interested in being a hard worker or self-improvement junkie.

I am deeply devoted to feeling good, taking bold action on the things I care about, and accepting the outcome that appears. I am getting good sleep, wonderful food, naps, walks, yoga. I am writing daily. Being with family and friends. I am observing people remembering they signed up for that and if they bump into me, it is for a common benefit.

I am willing to be hurt. To be rejected. I am willing to be an oddball. I feel the full range of the human experience and I return to homeostasis effortlessly. I really can't get it wrong, and neither can you. It is written. We are perfectly equipped for this adventure. It's all inside of us and we just might remember it while sitting in the pantry, walking through a field of flowers, or driving through a canyon.

And on the really shitty days when this all seems out of reach, we can-

Do something meaningful by making someone's day.

Do what we are good at for someone we care about.

We can cry until we are ready to play our cards.

What if no one could ever convince you that anything is wrong with your life as it is now? What if you never had to prove yourself to anyone ever again? And what if filled our lives in such a way that there was never again room for worry, self-doubt, envy, disease, and war?

Focus on *that* kind of magic.

ABOUT ADRIANA MONIQUE ALVAREZ

Adriana Monique Alvarez is the CEO and Founder of AMA Publishing. She is an unconventional visionary whose life and business was inspired by a decade of travel and volunteer work around the world. She is a USA Today best-selling author and a 19 time international bestselling author. She is an artist, photographer, and private chef for her husband Derek and two sons Sam and Grant. She is currently living in the middle of nowhere Colorado where she is renovating her grandparents home and learning how to homestead.

Website: www.amapublishing.co

2
ABI WILD ROSE

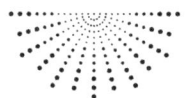

I was raised in a particular religion-dominant town. I was never encouraged to find the magic within. I'd been taught only to lean on the doctrine being programmed into us and not ask questions. To *stay small* and *stay obedient*. Hold only to blind faith and not see any perspective beyond the church's. I have always been the question-asker. I have never been one to just blindly follow the crowd.

As a child, I tried fully showing up for this religion. I tried to be a part of it all. If I didn't believe, wouldn't I be going to "Hell?" Surely I would be cast out of heaven and know no blessings or miracles in my life; that is what I had been told all of my life. For years I tried. I prayed, I cried; I begged to understand and have any of it truly resonate in my heart. It never did.

Many nights I laid in bed wondering why I was so broken. Why wouldn't God give me the sign that this church was true like he seemingly gave to every other peer and family member in my life? I did all the requirements at every age to be a member and made great effort to "choose the right." Wasn't I supposed to feel so renewed and whole again after doing all of these things and praying fervently to ask if these things were true like I had been taught? I didn't feel any of that and I never got confirmation. I felt nothing but confused and more disappointed that surely something was innately wrong with *me*.

My soul yearned for the *more* that I knew was meant for me. I got lost along the way and I didn't know where to start until many years later, but I subconsciously started laying that foundation as my life continued on and I gained new experiences.

Growing up in a small, rural town did have its perks of so much time in nature. When my family would go on our 3-day long bronco excursions or various campouts, I quickly learned that being under the stars and among the trees was the most healing remedy for my soul. The stars, planets, and nature have always been my safety and comfort. I found more peace in the arms of the Mamma Gaia than in any church I had ever been in. I found unconditional love from the stars and planets that surround us. Hearing the wind through the trees has always been my favorite lullaby. The sound of water dancing to and fro has forever been my heart's cadence.

When we weren't out in nature, as young as 8 years old I recall stacking various items around my dad's shed to climb on top of the roof and watch the stars for hours on end. Being up there with the stars alleviated so much of my anxiety, sadness, and loneliness as a kid. I have always found solace in the sky and in nature, even during my heaviest shadows. Being grounded out in nature surrounded by the sun, moon, and stars will forever be my safety and my peace.

My journey to my present-day Self has been far from an easy route. I carved a path through treacherous terrain to make it this far. There's been more than one occasion I shouldn't have made it through physically or even spiritually. For 15+ years I battled addictions to alcohol, cigarettes, and most any drug I could get my hands on.

I've woken up in the hospital on more than one occasion. I have accidentally overdosed and been brought back to life. I have tried and survived multiple attempts at opting myself out of my life. There have been (regrettably) countless times of making it home from the bar, the club, the party and having zero idea how I got there but somehow my car was outside. I've had a myriad of times I put myself around unsafe people while out of my mind and somehow made it through each unwise decision alive. I had too many to count wake-up calls. I never picked up the telephone line from the Universe in a hurry and took the hint that my lifestyle and my choices needed some redirection.

As I had made it through each of these times I genuinely shouldn't be alive, I started to slowly recognize that maybe I am unquestionably meant to be here. I had the yearning in my heart to find out why, to grab the magic I knew I held inside and to not waste any more of my precious time here.

However, having this realization was not the magic "fix-all" button for me. I have had to work through and process all of the shame and self-loathing I had accumulated from my choices during prior tumultuous times. At the time of my writing this (May 2024), I just freshly passed the 5-year mark of being free from hard drugs, nicotine, and alcohol and have been working daily at making better and more present-minded choices for myself. But even in the turn-around of my life choices, I have had toxic situations and people I have needed to sort through and release as I shed all of the layers of soul-muck I let myself accumulate while not living in divine alignment of my purpose here. I have noticed that every year sober I unlock old things that needed to resurface that I've had to face *soberly* and release from the newer versions of me. It has not been easy but oh so necessary.

As a brilliant therapist recently told me regarding a certain situation I was having to grow through and release, "You can't go walking into the woods for 10 years and expect to make it back out in a few days." He's right. I have had *work* to do. And still do in many ways as I learn to heal and forgive past versions of me. I think of these words he shared in all aspects of my growth. They have helped me give myself grace when it comes to unlearning and healing the traumas I have accumulated. I don't want to carry them into this new season and new version of me.

Tapping into a connection with my spiritual Self was a long process. I had enormous walls built up around all things concerning spiritual matters as an after-effect of religious trauma and for a long time considered myself to be an Atheist.

I started to research everything and anything religious or spiritual based from around 2007 and on just out of curiosity and to seek understanding. I slowly started to find bits that I resonated with and would release the things that didn't align with my soul. I still was not living a full-blown spiritually tuned-in lifestyle just yet, but I definitely was dipping my toes in the water.

While I was in the heaviest and thickest shadow of my addictions, I was using methamphetamines nearly every day. If I didn't have any, I was looking forward to the next time I would get to have more. I was not working steadily. I had quit my office job after getting into a toxic relationship and quickly started heavy drug usage. I would do odd jobs for people here and there to cover basic necessities and had picked up a serving job at a restaurant, but I was always so noticeably high that I would get very self-conscious of how people would look at me and how uncomfortable they would be by the size of my pupils and the state of mind I was in while I was scrambling around trying to keep it together, so I quit. "Lack" is quickly what my kids knew. "Lack" became my theme. I let any hardship feel like the Universe was against me; my narrative became that only bad things happened to me.

During this time, ironically enough, I was starting to tap more into my spiritual connection with my guides and angels. Throughout this period of my life, I actually started to pray again. Consistently. To speak with a higher power. To connect with Source and my guides and angels. I was simultaneously hating myself for not being able to climb out of the deep hole of addiction I had jumped down into while still trying to find my greater purpose and learn how to love myself and finally quit the poisons once and for all.

I longed so deeply to give my kids and myself a better life. When in the throes of addiction, I oftentimes felt so helpless to ever find the strength to succeed at finally pulling myself out of the clutch of poisons and reach any real goals.

What I have learned in my time here as Abi is that we all have guides and angels surrounding us; souls that agreed to help us during our time down here on Earth. We all have our own unique set of guides. They will do what they can to help us when we aren't outright reaching out to them or listening to their messages, but they can only do so much to help if we aren't paying attention to their communications and guidance.

We don't have to be a perfect person to have access to their loving help and input. That is why they agreed to help us- to get us through ALL times! *Especially* the times we may be feeling stuck in the muck; that is when we need guidance and love the very most! They hold the bigger picture ever-present for us. They have our backs. My guides and angels have had their hands FULL with me in this life. I wouldn't be here today if I didn't have such an amazingly supportive and protective spirit team around me.

I remember my first major conversation/heart-to-heart with my guides. I had just gotten into a (one-of-too-many) domestic dispute with my partner at the time and left my house needing to clear my head. I drove to a secluded spot amongst the cedar trees that overlooked an entire reservoir with our local mountain in the backdrop. I felt entirely crushed, heartbroken and so spiritually heavy. I was exhausted from the constant chaos and negativity that my life had become.

I sat there with my bare feet planted in the dirt and looked across the landscape; I was sobbing and trying to pull it together. I wanted to go home, not my physical home but my soul's home. I was not okay. I started talking to my guides out loud. I poured my entire heart out to them. I asked them so many questions and told them so many things. What my fears were. What I was disappointed in myself about. What I wanted to feel. How much I love my kids and wish I could do better. What I couldn't bear on my own anymore. Why am I still here? What is even the point anymore?

I told them every thought and asked them all of the questions; I held nothing back. At that moment of releasing it all, I felt their loving presence envelop me in the warmest, most comforting, and most powerful soul hug. I immediately acknowledged how beautifully surrounded by love and support I sincerely was. Talking to them often after this first magical conversation we had is quite honestly what kept me alive and helped me in the final years of my addiction cycle. I *know* I couldn't have done it without their love, guidance, and support.

In 2019 when I made this final attempt at sobriety, a new fire lit within. I finally "hit the wall" with my addictions and lifestyle. I knew if I didn't make better decisions for myself I was going to wind up in jail (again) or end up dead (for good this time). Every sober day fueled me to see how many more days I could go without using. I was determined to give my kids a better life, show them that absolutely anything is possible and that we do not have to be limited by "lack" any longer.

One part of my healing and finding my magic has been tapping into my inner child. Music and books were the two major life savers for me in my childhood and beyond to present day me. My Little Abi-self had big dreams and I let life derail them.

I always had a passion for music. I used to tape over the corners of the cassette tapes that we didn't use anymore so I could record myself over them. They were like my own personal music podcasts, of course well before podcasts were ever a thing. I wanted to write music, to be on stage and share the most vulnerable pieces of my heart in the brave, beautiful ways like I saw all of the talented "greats" do before me.

As I mentioned before, with the twists and turns of life, those dreams took the shelf. The last decade of my life has been me trying to get those dreams off of the shelf and back into my life focus. The most progress has been made towards them since getting sober but even in the thick of addiction leading up to sobriety I was trying to put myself out there and actually sing in front of others again.

I joined a band a few years ago and after showing myself I could be brave and do it, I told myself I wouldn't say no to musical opportunities anymore. During the various ups and downs of our band's journey, I made sure to always have my sights set on me taking flight and not letting myself down by letting fear hold me back from growth as a musician or keep me from opportunities that might help me evolve on this path. I have since learned to strive to put my focus on what I want to attract to me and not the poor attitude of others or obstacles thrown my way. Sometimes that is easier said than done, but every time I experience the days that are harder to find the magic I do see that I am making progress in learning to flow.

I believed in my band so much that I thought my big picture was making massive things happen in the band and that it was my endgame. As things got more rocky and as I realized the season with my band was about to be over, letting go of the outcome of the project I cared so deeply for and flowing allowed me to see that just because things don't turn out as planned or as I imagined they would, even better and more magical things line up for me.

Since leaving the band, I have embarked on doing music solo. This has been the ultimate challenge for me because I played the bass and was lead singer in the band, so now I am adjusting to being the guitar player while singing all alone on stage. These changes have already stretched me outside of my comfort zone in the best possible ways.

In taking that first step I have already made so many amazing musical connections and I am excited to see where this path leads. In one of my songs, I have written called "Note 2 Self" I say, "The risks that you take are the brave steps that lead you to freedom. Choices to make, choices can give or take from your growth."

I wrote that song in 2020 but it still resonates for me in new ways and reminds me to bravely make purposeful choices.

I have learned that praying/talking to my guides as often as possible is the best way for me to stay in connection with my highest Self. They give me so much clarity and when there are times I am not supposed to know the answers to my question just yet, they bring comfort and help me transmute the confusion or sadness I may feel. That also goes for helping me through the moments when things turn out differently than I envisioned.

I write affirmations often and I have learned to be very intentional with my energy and where I spend it. Not every day will look and feel the best but that doesn't mean there is no wisdom to learn or blessings to receive.

With each new season of my life, I am learning magic in new forms. This current season, I am learning there is magic in surrender. I am releasing what I feel any outcome should look like, even when Spirit strongly says something is meant for me, but the timing is not right. I am learning patience and the importance of self-love and self-care. I am training to allow myself the absolute surrender into the unknown of what's to come and trust that I am divinely loved and protected. Always, in all ways.

I must wrap this up, so in conclusion- I am so grateful for the opportunity to get to work on this chapter. Writing has been another passion of mine since I was a little girl. Having my first step in that direction be getting to work on such a beautiful, inspiring project has been such an honor. I have stretched myself out of my comfort zone to evolve by showing up for this opportunity.

I have learned through experience that the space beyond my comfort zone has always been and I know will continue to always be the space I perpetually learn to spread my wings and fly.

Please remember to hydrate, to breathe, and to know that you are so loved. Be good to each other and be good to your Self.

Much love,
Abi Wild Rose

ABOUT ABI WILD ROSE

Abi Wild Rose is an alchemist and intuitive healer that is here to help raise the vibrations on Earth. She is an aspiring Musician, Spiritual Life Coach, End-of-Life Doula and budding Sobriety Coach, Motivational Speaker and Author. She is a mother to two beautiful girls, Phoenix and Phaye. She was raised in a rural town in Southeast Utah and moved all over the country at 18. She came back to her hometown in 2010 and underwent major karmic lessons. She learned to overcome addictions and has been on her self-love and healing journey for quite some time now. She's currently relocating to the Western Slope of Colorado and is ready for new beginnings.

Facebook: www.facebook.com/Abi.Wild.Rose

3
ALICIA MARIE ANZALDI

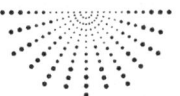

QUANTUM WITNESS

When I first found the healing work that I do, I knew it was the work I was here to do. I had zero understanding of frequency/vibration other than a cursory awareness. But I felt and saw amazing results that did not make any clinical sense, so I had to trust the work.

Trust it. This felt exactly like having an allergy for me.

Within a few days of starting work with clients, I became aware that there was more information present in the room than I was told by the doctor and client. Sometimes it felt crowded. Like my shoulders were pressed against on both sides by others who were helping. Sometimes there was just extra understanding without verbal input.

A client in my first week came for their first session of therapy. I understood instantly via what I can only describe as a snapshot/polaroid that he likely had pancreatic cancer. He hadn't spoken yet but then mentioned belly pain, fatigue, and more concerning symptoms. It is outside of my scope of practice to diagnose or to make recommendations, so I encouraged him to go to the ER immediately and ask for his pancreas to be scanned. His wife confirmed to me the next day that my intuition was correct.

Situations like this continued for several years. However, they grew in detail and started to include generally recognizable energies such as angels, religious figures, ancestors, animals... It turns out it really WAS crowded in a treatment room! It became natural for more channeled information to come through for a client – often medical or related emotional/energetic understanding that would help them get to the root of their issues. Often the visual representations were deeply / personally significant to them.

In 2018, I was teaching at a hospital in Flagstaff, AZ, and had planned to spend the next day in Sedona hiking, crystal shopping, and thrifting. I was nervous about teaching lymphatics to a group of cancer doctors – some of it was my material. I have no medical degree and didn't finish my associate degree in favor of supporting myself.

I arrived at the hospital early and watched a group of crows having a meeting across the parking lot. I love crows. All birds, but crows... they're a favorite. I wanted one to come and hang out near me. But I had no offerings, so just thought about how nice it would be. One separated from the group and did a slow, short flight over to the curb next to my car. He stayed good while. It vaguely occurred to me that maybe it was a coincidence that he did that. I felt grateful. The class was a success, and the therapy is still a part of the breast cancer standard of care for that group of hospitals.

Upon waking the next day to drive to Sedona, I felt a deep stillness. It was still kind of dark at 6:30, but there was a perfect full moon getting ready to set. I decided to take the mountain road instead of the interstate into Sedona, and as I left the metro area of Flagstaff, the hair on my arms stood up. This sensation intensified over the drive. Once I reached the point where there were mountains/landforms along the road, I started to hear something. There were layers to this sound... beautiful hollow ringing tones, and a quiet but heavy oscillating wind noise. The ringing made me have an awareness of minerals and crystals in the land around me. There was visual input with this – grids of geometric light, waves, pictures, and more.

While I do technically have synesthesia, I also have no natural lenses in my eyes. So, I have access to slightly more of the light spectrum than standard. I am used to a thin "overlay" of this at all times. I've heard it's like doing psychedelics, but this is just me, raw. What I saw this day looked tangible.

As I drove closer to Sedona, this feeling intensified. My only choice was to drive past it. I was able to stop the car 12 miles south of Sedona. That's when I could finally hear/see properly again. Once parked, I saw what I can only describe as rainbow clouds. I took photos with my cell phone to keep the memory. They were iridescent but also made a very thick rainbow. Anyone who knows me knows I LOVE rainbows. Or iridescence of any kind. It makes me deliriously happy.

Once I came back from that trip and went back to work, things started to change. There started to be more visual information available on clients' bodies. I had noticed some consistencies across clients regarding certain medical conditions providing quantifiable information that was consistent across clients or conditions.

Then things intensified, as I started to be able to understand more about someone's emotional state in a very detailed way. I became aware of the pathways of illness/conditions and started to be able to help people piece together the more subtle parts of their conditions. Including the energetic or emotional connection to their physical body. Information during sessions started to become so organized and reliable that it started to unnerve others and myself. Literal note cards of words written in block letters with a sharpie is how this looks during a session.

Going to the grocery store or the gym became complicated. I'm over here trying to pick out strawberries. I DO NOT need to know how much you regret your life choices, sir. I started to lose control of my day-to-day, as things became overwhelming. I turned to 3 important people in my life: my eye doctor, my psychiatrist, and a friend who is a brilliant doctor. I shared everything that happened. My eye doctor told me his best friend has the same issues and is a gifted eye surgeon. My psychiatrist asked me why I would even see her because she hasn't kicked her alcoholism yet, and I said "Well... I know that, but you are literally learning coping skills, which allows me to just read what they are like a note card."

My doctor friend put me in touch with another doctor friend who has similar abilities, who encouraged me to take energy work classes, and is a dear friend now.

I learned that basically none of the "techniques" matter. It isn't what you're doing with your hands, it's your visualization, intention, and ability to stay present + focused as well as an open channel. It matters that you command the space. Clear it and instruct it to release what needs to be, while still being a safe, protected place. Your electromagnetic energy will broadcast what it needs to. Electro, meaning thoughts. Magnetic energy is emotions. It's why your thoughts and emotions affect those around you, and vice versa. Think about places you feel the presence of others, or maybe just "pressure" when you're around others. Your heart? Your throat? Stomach? Head? Low back? All of those have different resonances, however, the physical cells vibrate differently due to others' energy and will feel out of tune with yours if they are ill or having negative emotions, or actively choosing disharmony in their lives. Your cells/organs will try to tune theirs up, which drains you.

At its core, magic is about being a quantum witness – open and present to receive. That means you've created a space for it. Magic lives in the pause. The quiet moment in between breaths; in between thoughts. It lives in the array of tiny, liquid rainbow beams that make up one small ray of sunlight. When you can get there and exist in that, you are that magic. Be the light that shines through the petal of a magenta and yellow rose. That color becomes the true sovereign sound of that flower because the light activates the water in that one petal. The water inside that plant is what broadcasts the sound of the sun to make that color vibration sing. Be that light by stopping to truly see it and appreciate it. When you ingest that color, you are witnessing it at its highest expression. That is where the magic is physically located – deep appreciation for beauty, kindness, anything positive. Go all the way into it to appreciate its worth. When you can stay in that place mentally for sustained amounts of time, you have created space in your life for magic and it arrives.

About 2 weeks after the experience in Sedona, I was having difficulty managing the gifts that I was given, even after great advice. I was taking some time in my workspace to do therapy on myself and some meditation. I decided to ask for help. I asked that all messages be crystal clear and relevant only to what the client is asking for. I asked that the information always be pleasant and beautiful, even if it's challenging news, and that I can only see information if something useful can be done with it. I asked for complete clarity, and complete separation from this ability unless I chose to access it in the moment. My veterinarian had recently spoken to me about only asking for positive outcomes. Focusing on what isn't wanted or what has already happened tends to create more problems. I asked for these things from a place of true surrender – I was really struggling.

I noticed a change in the sessions right away. A lightness. The energetic focus changed. Conditions started to shift for people. I started to book more energetically literate clients, people who wanted help processing the deep work of psychotherapy, and people who wanted to consciously receive a level of energetic work that was more than just physical detox.

I had recently met someone who went on to become the equivalent of my spiritual godmother. I met Irina* because another client referred me to her. She offers a modality called Aura Soma, as well as many other practices. Color is sacred to me. It tells me every detail of what I want to know about something. It is my favorite language. Aura Soma is about frequency and the pairing of colors and numbers, and much more. On the wall of her office is a backlit shelf that had

---

* *While this is a true story, client's name was changed to protect their identity.*

over 100 bottles of color/frequency. At my appointment time, when I tried to walk into her office, I had to back out for a second to allow my senses to adjust to the symphony in her office.

She sat back in her chair and looked at me in a way that I'm now become familiar with from other individuals with abilities like mine. A relief. The slow exhale. The tuning of fields. Shared memory. A sistar. I remember you. "Arcturian," she said. I handed her my card. I had been doing consulting and training with Arcturus Star Products at the time. "Yes," I said.

I could see the shadow in her left breast. It wasn't opaque, but it was unmistakable. I also knew based on the red X appearing plain as day next to her that I was not allowed to tell her yet. She did a reading for me, then some channeling. It was all beyond accurate, yet eye-opening. When I was ready to leave, I knew she would call me for assistance.

Several months later, she did.

I had been teaching that weekend and am usually feeling like a used plastic bag at the end of the 1st day. I got a text from Irina that she was in crisis and needed a visit with me right away. Normally I won't even respond to texts on a teaching weekend, but I knew I needed to help her. She arrived with her husband, a gifted doctor. I had only met him briefly. She got settled on the table and he sat next to us, almost too close for my comfort – kind of in my space but right on the edge. I let it go and allowed myself to feel his support. He seemed anxious.

About 15 minutes into the session, I was working on her left underarm with my laser. I had just recently been exploring bioresonance and was shown to use some blue obsidian chips alongside her underarm. I placed them near her on the table and continued working. Her husband was to my right, about eye level with her.

As I was clearing, there started to be a watery, white/holographic ribbon that appeared on her chest, from about her right underarm across to the left side, then down into her left underarm and off her, through the crystals and illuminating them, then winding down the wooden leg of the table into the floor. I had not seen anything like this yet. It was very beautiful, and I couldn't help staring at it.

After a minute, the edges stayed beautiful, but the majority of it changed. There weren't pictures, but there was color and sound. The sound was a multitude of pain. The colors stayed relatively pretty, but I understood what they were. It was an energetic record of all the pain her soul had experienced thus far. After a few minutes, I looked at her husband next to me, wondering if he had any idea what in the actual world was going on here. I wondered if he could see or sense anything going on. He continued to just gaze lovingly at her, so I looked back.

There was a loud gasp from her, then a deep smell. She had her eyes closed and writhed somewhat. While she was facing away, I leaned back so she couldn't see my hand, and pointed directly where I could see the tumor, and made eye contact with her husband. He nodded in understanding. After that moment, the session changed again. Everything went back to normal. The ribbon disappeared. The crystals stopped lighting up, and I continued on with the physical work.

Once she stood up to go to the bathroom, I started to clean up. I was trying to make this all right in my mind. What did I just see? Did this actually happen? I haven't even had one gummy today.... All the thoughts trying to get me to disbelieve. Her husband sat forward and said, "They made it holographic so you would look at it the whole time. Your job is to witness."

"So... you could see that? All of it? The cancer....?" I asked. He nodded. She came out right after. I wanted to tell her. The red X appeared. Not my place. But why make me aware of it in front of her husband?

She had testing very shortly after, following her own intuition. Her husband was meant to know to support her to help her get to the place where she felt safe to explore treatment. So much of dealing with cancer is about conscious decision-making based on physical resources and what is best. It is incredibly complicated and the more input from others, the more confusing it gets. It's a very solitary journey in the beginning, and the foundation matters. She needed to be ready to receive that information and it had to be on her terms, in her language. What happened was meant to build her support system and validate her later when she had doubts. Her recovery was miraculous and with minimal issues.

That was just the beginning of what I now refer to as quantum witnessing.

So many more magical things have happened. I witness miracles daily in my practice. Miracles over something so small in the grand scheme of life, but monumental for an energetically aligned person. The type of depth that goes in a diary, but it plays out in front of me like a metaphysical filmstrip. Focusing on the magic is the easy part. It's staying in it that creates challenges. That's when you go back to the sunlight coming through a rose.

Staying in the magic takes work. Rededication. Commitment. Belief. But most of all, it takes choosing joy, beauty, gratitude, gentleness, and play. Living like this requires humor. Understanding why an abusive person does what they do, then understanding the pain behind their life, and so on can be a very dark, real place. It's challenging to see all that in a split second. But that level of ability comes with the reward of zero filter, which means just when I think I'm crazy, Jesus will appear to a client in a pale pink bathrobe with a satin sash, burgundy sleep pants, bunny slippers, and a cup of coffee. I was so glad I didn't have to describe this scenario to the receiver, and they vocalized it instead! The most fun part is that my first client the next day, who is a devout follower of Jesus, showed up in a pale pink shirt and maroon pants the next day. I had to "sneeze" and go out in the hall for a minute to gather myself. I often see (regular) Jesus when working with her.

Doing "healing" work is the honor of my life. I truly do nothing. Truly. I just witness.

You are the magic. Just allow yourself to see it and receive it. The distance between you and magic is your thoughts only. Go dance. Play outside. Be in harmony with yourself. That is, you focusing on the magic because you are in it, and you are it.

ABOUT ALICIA MARIE ANZALDI

Alicia Marie Anzaldi is the Founder of Integrative Lymphatic Techniques and provides electro lymphatic drainage and intuitive development in the 4 Corners area of Colorado, and the Chicago Suburbs, and provides online training for both. She has spent 13 years providing lymph therapy, and 8 years training others in this modality. She developed Integrative Lymphatic Techniques in 2023 in collaboration with Hope4Cancer, and spent 1 year as Vice President of Arcturus Star Products to assist with transition. She is a writer, singer, artist, and dog mom, always ready to have an adventure in nature with friends or her partner.

Facebook:
www.facebook.com/integrativelymphatictechniques

4
AMY DANGER

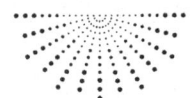

When you think of the word magic, what comes to mind? Is it a person dressed in slacks, a button-up shirt, with face paint, and a top hat with a wand? Or is it about the big moments that stick out in your life that are unbelievable and you didn't ever think would happen? Is it being celebrated by feeling the magic of the earth, elements, and seasons? Or is it what some people think of as coincidence?

Personally, I believe it is all of those and more.

One of my magical moments in my life was accomplishing a goal, or more of a dream I had always had. Since I was about 12 years old I wanted to drive a semi. I grew up in a time of the Knights of the Road. Beautiful, large trucks with lights everywhere, what could be better than road-tripping for a living?

But just like most of us do I got caught up in life and went in a completely different direction out of high school.

In my 40's the old dream I had had once upon a time, had come back. I was driving a school bus daily which I enjoyed, absolutely loved the kids on my bus, but it was not the big, beautiful semi and there was very little "road tripping" to be had while driving a school bus, except for the occasional out of town sports competition I would drive some of the teams to. I also had a very hard time realizing I was in charge of 50-plus beautiful souls on both runs I had every day. Watching cars run my red lights on a continual basis and getting angry out of fear that one day one of those little souls I was responsible for could possibly be getting hurt was too much. I started looking around at driving companies that paid for my official training, and off I went to training and gained my CDL A and off to on-the-road training. When I came home from the over-the-road training I was mentally beat, missing my kids and grandkids, and being home with my boyfriend. I decided maybe I was wrong about the job.

Fast forward about a year after coming off the road and a good friend of mine was working for an amazing company that was local to the Four Corners area and went coast to coast. Told me to give his boss a call and that there was a good possibility that they may be hiring, and I did just that and sadly the transportation manager said he didn't think that they would be hiring anytime soon but to come over and put my application in so he would have it just in case something opened up.

The next day I went to the company and applied for the job, my application process turned into about an hour and a half, which was crazy! Little did I know it was filling out my application, the interview, and getting the job before I knew I had gotten the job. He asked me a very important question, "Do you feel ok going to New England on your first run?" I asked when that would be, and he said in two days only because Thanksgiving was the next day, and I would leave the following day. I said sure. Shrugged my shoulders and thought, "What the hell?" I had the training and felt confident but had not been over the road in a semi completely alone, without a trainer, and I had never been to New England. I am not one to back down from anything and just went with it.

I went all the way across the country and only panicked once when I saw the New York City skyline from New Jersey. I called my coworker and the only thing I wanted to know was whether or not I had to go "over there" because at the time I had not realized I was looking at NYC.

    I don't ever have anxiety, but I almost did at that moment. I have been in big cities and lived in big cities but what I was looking at was beyond all that. Luckily he said not this time, I was super happy about that. I finished all my deliveries, got the backhaul, and headed home.

    I was very lucky to get the run I did, it was one of the longest in the company which was more money, but it also meant I would be gone all but about 8 days per month. But I loved doing one run to New England and then coming home for time off and then leaving and going to Southern California on my next run and this pattern continued for the entire time I worked for that company. The other reason I was so lucky to get that same run was the fact that my friend ran the same run and was always opposite of me, so anytime I was unsure about where to go I would call him, and he would walk me into where I needed to go for my deliveries. The interesting thing about this actual company was that I unloaded my orders, and I was delivering to malls and outlet malls. I learned to get a semi into locations I never thought possible, but in all fairness, I still cannot parallel park my car.

    I got home from my first run and thought to myself, I am either crazy or just stupid to do that run completely by myself for the first solo trip in a semi but then I thought no, you are neither of those. I knew eventually I would have to do that run so I just got it done and over the years did end up going into NYC and conquering that fear along with the big bridges (I don't like bridges) and going to Southern California for the first time as well. I learned on that first trip how to time my deliveries, so I didn't get stuck in rush hour traffic ever again.

    I truly loved driving semi and was in very good health unloading all my cargo all the time. I had more of a local dedicated run that just ran from coast to coast. I wouldn't have traded it for anything. My magical moment in all of this was accomplishing a dream I had for myself for so many years, meeting my fear head-on and just going with the flow, knowing I wouldn't let it stop me was exhilarating. I was a woman trucker!

My dad had also driven truck for the Army and transported hazardous material, so for him to see his little girl driving that big semi made him smile and he was happy. He even gave me his tire thumper and some of his trucking maps etc. I was glad I have those memories with him before he passed away.

Years later I was diagnosed with stage 3 breast cancer and unfortunately couldn't drive through all my surgeries and treatments. That is what took me off the road. I have fully recovered and that is another story within itself but not to be told just yet. This was all about the magic I felt and found within myself in that truck.

So, if you're thinking about chasing a dream DO IT!!

ABOUT AMY DANGER

Amy Danger lives in the Four Corners area of Colorado, she has been in Colorado since childhood and is originally from Illinois. She enjoys the outdoor activities the area has to offer and loves the culture in the area. She loves her family and pets and spends as much time with all of them as she can.

    She is also the owner and creator of Awen Designs by Amy, where she makes wire-wrapped jewelry and also offers lapidary services. The business is fairly new and not her sole income as of yet, but she hopes one day to make her small business and hobby into her main income. She is currently working on her yoga teacher training and hopes to be able to share her love of yoga with many people.

        Website: www.awendesignsbyamy.org
        Email: emailawendesignsbyamy@gmail.com

5
CATHERINE CABRERA

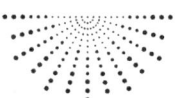

When we're kids, we view the world through a lens of imagination and wonder for the world around us—our dreams and aspirations are part of the endless opportunities ahead of us! Naturally, as we grow up, that imagination and wonder is pushed into a box in the name of being realistic. Looking back, my imagination and wonder were watered down earlier than I would hope for a child; however, I've come to realize why that is: from a young age, I was identified as 'mature,' not because I wanted to be but because I had to be. Because of my life experiences, instead of excitement and curiosity for what was ahead of me, my imagination morphed into fear and anxiety of what could be.

Watching my stepfather shapeshift from a loving and caring person to an absolute monster was a major turning point in my life. I had grown to trust him and feel safe with him in my life, but when his youngest daughter graduated high school, his attitude toward me changed. When my mom refused to leave me to run away with him, things went downhill very quickly. I was in my sophomore year of high school, putting me at sixteen years old, when he became emotionally abusive toward me and my mom. He'd throw away food so I couldn't eat when I got home from work, completely disregard my existence when I entered the room, and indirectly make it known that I was viewed as a burden in his eyes. Along with the typical teenager angst, I became very quiet—I isolated, hurt myself, and wanted nothing more than to feel like I mattered, but I believed the narrative he fed me.

I internalized that narrative to the point that I developed an eating disorder—starving myself because I believed that I didn't deserve to eat, and if I did, I had to burn it all off, no matter what it took. This lasted close to six years, but like my imagination shifted, so did my eating disorder. I recovered and did the work to gain back the necessary weight; however, my attention shifted to what became an unhealthy relationship. Feeling like I wasn't good enough, I spent my days anxiously waiting for the day he'd leave or find someone 'better.' The kicker? That's exactly what happened—I found out he had been cheating on me and when I would confront him, I somehow was the problem. He'd yell and tell me I was crazy, driving me to have panic attacks almost daily despite both of us knowing the truth. Several months later, he moved in with her.

You'd think that was my lowest point, and at that time, I thought it was too. A year later, I reunited with someone I had been friends with in college, as we were now attending the same graduate program. We spent time catching up, and he learned everything that had happened since I last saw him. With time, we started dating. Looking back, there were huge red flags that I missed—and I mean A LOT—but I also believed I deserved to be treated like I didn't matter. It had become normal for me by that point, so I failed to see them for what they were.

After being gradually broken down over the next two years, shit hit the fan. He went into the military, and I supported him through all of it, despite it meaning my dreams for the future being shattered. While he was at bootcamp, I learned what became the catalyst for the downward spiral the next six months were—he had been cheating on me. Everything came flooding back to me: refusing to post anything about us on social media, shifting everything to be at the fault of my past and anxiety, making everything about what he wanted to do, the constant jabs at my insecurities with the cover of being a joke... all of it spanning back to the very beginning. He denied everything, of course, but as the next few months progressed, the truth became undeniable. He requested we take a break from the relationship at this point, which blindsided me entirely, and then ignored me for the next five days, refusing to say anything to me despite knowing I was in probably the darkest depression I've ever experienced. My eating disorder resurfaced, I couldn't work, I couldn't even leave my bed. The man I had trusted with my past and my heart, used all of it against me without any remorse.

I anticipated what came next, but it's something no person should be used to—he claimed I was crazy, shifted the blame onto me, and accused me of being emotionally abusive. All the while, his mother posted a photo of him and another girl on social media with all the comments reading "what a beautiful couple!" It was in that moment, and the moments following, my whole perspective changed. He continued to deny everything, despite the immense amount of evidence I had, and I blocked him—the person I loved desperately. His social media accounts, his phone number, everything, and I went the step further of blocking his parents too because they played a role in stringing me along too, as I later learned.

Something in that moment finally made it all click: I didn't deserve to be treated like dirt. I *refused* to be treated that way anymore. I vividly remember having this epiphany that said, "what could happen if we came up with a new story?" It was at that moment, I decided I was going to let it all go. Did it hurt? Absolutely! But it hurt more living the same narrative over and over again and being made to feel like my existence didn't matter. For the first time in my life, I was going to put myself first. I was going to discover and abide by my own beliefs, values, and dreams. I spent my life afraid of being viewed as not good enough by the people I loved and cared for the most, and I refused to be afraid anymore. I refused to keep living in fear.

With that, I wanted to start over completely—give myself a blank slate. That same week my relationship crumbled at my feet, I decided to open my own virtual therapy practice. I built it from the ground up, with the help of my sister-in-law, in a single week, which allowed me to leave the practice I had been working at through that relationship. All of my clients from my previous site decided to move to my practice with me, giving me the confidence boost I desperately needed. That alone told me that I was doing something right, and I was finally doing it for me!

With this newfound mentality toward myself and the world around me, it felt as though everything started to change for the better. Approaching the world with curiosity, wonder, and compassion seemed to shift everything! I moved into my first apartment, my business was doing well, my mental health drastically improved with time ... what more could I have asked for?

As time went on, I decided to venture into the dating world—a realm I had never experienced before. It was an adventure, to say the least, but I honored myself in ways I had never done before. When I got mixed signals from someone, I'd confront them and acknowledge what I was feeling. If someone ghosted me or expressed disinterest, I simply moved on. I found myself not buying into my previous narrative anymore, and truly believed in myself and what I had to offer as a partner. It certainly crossed my mind, as is natural after twenty years of living it, but I chose to allow myself to be authentic and genuine rather than shapeshift into who I thought someone else wanted me to be.

A few months in, I met someone who would become incredibly special and important to me. He's someone who also sees the world with a kind heart and feeds into my wonder; he's the epitome of what I've always wanted in a partner and a relationship. He demonstrates authentic care and love for me, including practicing patience and compassion when my trauma or anxiety resurfaces. You know, the first healthy relationship after a traumatic one is always the hardest!

As I've fostered this new narrative, this belief that I'm worth it and I have a purpose in this world, I've gotten the sense that the Universe felt the shift in me too. Several opportunities have come my way that I never would've imagined for myself! I write mental health-related articles for a well-known online magazine, I've authored an international bestseller and I'm in the process of being included in two other books, I was honored with the opportunity to be on the front cover of the magazine I write articles for, and I was interviewed on Business Innovators Radio! How cool is that?!

With all of the amazing opportunities I've been granted and been a part of in recent years, I find it important to look back on my life and spend time sitting with my younger self. What would I say to her? What did she need to hear? Of all the things I would want to say to comfort her, it all comes down to one piece of advice: *don't be afraid to see the beauty in the world*. Even in the darkest of times, I can look back and see moments of beauty—glimmers of my true self wanting to come out, but I was too afraid to let the world see her. I understand this fear now, the desire to keep something away from the countless people who threw sticks and stones my way—I wanted to hold onto *something* that they couldn't take away. But in reality, I was keeping her caged and miserable in the name of safety.

There's beauty all around us—sometimes it's harder to find, I'll admit that, but I know it's there! Take a minute to sit with yourself—think about the people and moments around you that bring you joy, a sense of belonging, opportunity, that warm and fuzzy feeling. Write them down and keep them somewhere you frequent. This could be your bedside table, bathroom mirror, the back of your bedroom door, wherever you'll see it on a daily basis. *Why am I doing this?* These are various demonstrations of magic in your life! And guess what? You are a source of magic for the people in your life too!

Now, creating and living by this narrative does not mean disregarding turbulent experiences in your life; they are just as valid as those of excitement. It can be easy to fall into the mindset that life is hard and shit sucks because, realistically, it really does sometimes! But I'll share something with you that I share with my therapy clients: it's the mixture of experiences and emotions that allows us to fully appreciate the magic around us. There's a concept in the therapy world—probably not exclusive to it—referenced as dialectics, which basically means one experience can elicit multiple, seemingly conflicting responses simultaneously. Think of going on a rollercoaster or watching a scary movie—you probably feel both scared and excited, or you're nervous but love the experience at the same time. With that in mind, our outlook on life can be approached the same way. Life can be difficult and overwhelming AND magical and beautiful.

It took me a long time, and I mean a LONG time, to come to that realization, and to be transparent, it took me getting fed up with feeling broken and unwanted. I had to get to that point where I was looking in the mirror, knowing it was a reflection but I didn't recognize the person staring back at me. She was miserable and desperate for something different. I already knew what the outcome was if I kept doing what I was doing, but the hope of living a happier life motivated me to try something different, to try buying into a new narrative.

It was easily the best decision of my life. I surrounded myself with people I love, who also love and support me. I found myself being pushed toward certain opportunities and away from others in a way I can only describe as the Universe guiding me toward what was meant for me. Whether it was in my career, relationships, opportunities, where to live, everything! Hell, the fact that I'm featured in this book is a prime example: I came across a post in a Facebook group about the cover being revealed and something about the cover drew me in—seriously, it's gorgeous! I had made a comment or liked the post, and I was connected with the woman who was in charge of inviting authors to join the project. She described the opportunity and what her vision was and, I know how cheesy this is going to sound, I felt this warmth in my chest and my heart told me to go for it. I had no clue what I was going to write about, but at that moment, I knew this was something for me—I could feel the magic in the conversation with her and every time I sat down to spill my thoughts onto the pages you're reading now.

The freedom that has come with my narrative shift continues to blow my mind every single day. Recognizing the beauty and magic in my genuine self and sharing that with the world around me has fostered an unprecedented level of confidence for me. I can approach the world with love, compassion, and empathy without fear of it being exploited. Yes, I do experience anxiety from my past experiences, but I've also learned how to communicate and let others support me in a way that I never would've allowed previously. In my expression of love and curiosity for others and life as a whole, it's given me the opportunity to welcome those into my life too!

Focusing on the beauty and magic in my life has granted me the ability and opportunity to welcome into my life everything I always wanted—an abundance of love, creativity, openness, support, and even more magical moments!

ABOUT CATHERINE CABRERA

Catherine Cabrera, founder of *Inner Strength Counseling & Coaching, LLC*, is a mental health therapist and a Mindset & Empowerment Coach, specializing in the treatment of anxiety, eating disorders, people-pleasing, and perfectionism. Catherine helps her clients build healthy relationships with themselves and their emotions through curiosity and compassion. Catherine is also an Executive Contributor for *Brainz Magazine*, sharing her expertise and knowledge on various aspects of mental health and healing, was honored as a 2023 Brainz 500 Global Award recipient, and co-authored the international bestseller *My Mess is My Message II*, a culmination of inspiring stories of women who found purpose and prosperity through adversity in their lives.

Catherine is passionate about her work in the mental health field, both inside and out of the therapy and coaching spaces. She operates her own blog on her website with the intention of providing resources and education on anxiety-related mental health challenges to help those who don't have the resources to utilize professional services.

Website: www.innerstrengthcounselingllc.net
Email: ccabrera.isc@gmail.com
Articles: www.brainzmagazine.com/executive-contributor/catherine-cabrera
Instagram: www.instagram.com/catherinecabrera.isc

6
MADIA SMITH

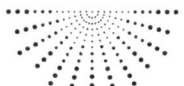

𝒲hen I was invited to share a chapter in this book, I responded with an immediate, "Yes! Of course." My body answered before my brain could catch up. The decision to write was instant and unquestioned. But when I reread the subtitle for *Focus on the Magic*, I was a bit bewildered and somewhat deflated.

"Leaders of the new earth?" I am no leader and, to be honest, I doubt the existence of magic most days. However, I realized that, despite my occasional shitty moods and anxiety, I have a continual sense of the extraordinary reality of life.

How a seed becomes a tree, a gosling hatches from an egg, and the sun warms our planet from 94 million miles away is all magic when you consider the intricacies of biology and physics that must be so precisely perfect in order for any of it to happen.

We often equate knowledge with what can be measured, dismissing anything unquantifiable as unreal or unreliable. However, there exists a collective recognition of unknowing. We all sense that there is something profound about existence that cannot be captured by words, proofs, or logical thought. Every scientific explanation can be followed with the question, "Yes, but why?"

If we ask this question enough times, we inevitably arrive at the unsettling state of unknowing. The purpose of anything, or everything, becomes unknowable to the logical mind. Yet, on the other side of this unknowingness lies a Knowing. When explanations fall short, the frantic left brain pauses, and in that stillness, the under-used parts of our brain awaken to the realization of something else - something infinite and beyond comprehension.

I will not try to prove the existence of God because such proof is impossible.

God cannot be proven because God is not a being that is definable, measurable, or understandable. Within Catholic and orthodox theology, God is not thought of as "A Being" at all - but rather as *Being Itself* (or existence itself: *ipsum esse*).

God, as Being, is both immediately knowable and infinitely unknowable. And if the term "God" troubles you, let us simply ask: what is Being?

Since Being cannot be properly defined, measured, or understood, this mystery of "Is-ness" is what many have called "God." But I am not a philosopher, and this topic deserves a level of robustness that is beyond the scope of this essay.

You are here to read stories about magic. If I still have your attention, pause and ask yourself, "What do I think magic is?"

Do you have your answer?

In this chapter, I'm going to explore the idea that "magic" is the part of Being that we have not been able to explain - and perhaps is unexplainable. The parts of the world and our existence that defy logic. The moments when the universe completely overwhelms our brain. The place where our own depth overwhelms our brain. The place where answers to the "whys" and "hows" dry up.

Magic is where our beingness reveals who and what we are. As we get in touch with the miracle of our very existence, we begin to fill the "God-shaped hole" that sits behind every rational explanation.

You may have been drawn to this book because you sense there is magic within you and seek proof of the unprovable. The wondrous thing about magic is that even the attempt to explain it logically makes it more magical.

Take, for example, the universe. When you gaze into the sky, you are looking into the past. The light from most of the visible celestial bodies took many, many years to reach us. Thousands, billions. We can use powerful telescopes to, quite literally, *look back in time* at events that are no longer happening because it has taken *that* long for the light to reach us.

This is a well-accepted fact, and yet the implications of it are mind-bending. If we can see something that is no longer in existence, then there necessarily are things that exist but we can't yet see.

Time itself is a feature of the physical universe. It, along with other aspects of our reality, does not exist without the physical. When we try to conceptualize what was "before" the Big Bang, the exercise is futile because the concept of "before" does not exist without time.

There is only Being, only unknowing; things our physical brains cannot grasp because we live in a physical world governed by physical laws.

My brain is working hard at wrapping itself around a concept that, the more I dissect it, becomes increasingly wild and unimaginable.

Now, take this concept but zoom in on the individual experience:

I don't think there is a truly knowable answer to the ultimate "Being" question: "Why am I here?" but there may be an answer to "What am I here for?"

When you start down the rabbit hole of this question, you must reconnect with your being-ness. You arrive at that part of you that is so deeply *you*, that it defies explanation. It's the same exercise of contemplating what existed "before" the birth of the universe.

What parts of you existed before *your* birth?

As we embrace the inexplicable aspects of our existence, we

discover this thing we have nebulously and imperfectly defined as magic.

Since you're here for a story, I'll give a personal example.

Over the past year or so, I started reconnecting with my spiritual side. I've always felt "tapped in," but I hit the mute button for several years after a "dark night of the soul" where I felt like there was nothing and no one - except myself - pulling me through it.

In addition to soul-searching, meditation, and examining my mindset, I started listening to various spiritual and woo-themed podcasts. One of them offered a chance to win a psychic reading if I left a review, so on a whim, I did.

I'll preface this story by coming out of the spiritual closet a little and admitting that I have always sensed a presence around me. Angels, spirit guides, ancestors, God; I don't know, but something beyond my own energy. Whoever or whatever, I often talk to them like a pissed-off teenager. I feel annoyed with them most of the time, annoyed that - if they are real - communication is subpar.

Where's that experience of unconditional, transcendent love I hear about? Never felt it.

Anyway, I had just experienced the loss of two pets back-to-back. The second was a beautiful white goose entrusted to me by her rescuer. She developed an abscess in her oil gland, and we were treating her daily with oral antibiotics, debridement, and topical solutions. The vet thought her prognosis was good, and she seemed to be making positive progress.

Then, out of nowhere, she became lethargic. Within hours, she passed away with my husband and I watching her last breaths, as I prayed, internally screamed, and begged for any higher power to help her. I saw the light go out of her eyes which, if you have not watched death come, is not just a figure of speech. There is a light in the eyes with life, and then they are dark.

I was sad and angry. Beneath that, I was frustrated by the lack of cosmic apology for the abandonment I felt during my soul's dark night. If there is a God, if there are angels, spirits, and a higher self existing on a non-physical plane outside the bounds of time, they didn't go out of their way to announce their presence.

So, in my mind's eye, I marched up to my angels and yelled at them.

My eloquent diatribe went something like this:

"Fuck you."

Silence.

I tried again, less profane but angrier. "*Why?*"

Then I considered - not for the first time - that there was nothing except for me. Just an internal monologue in my brain, me talking to myself.

"*If you exist, say something!*"

And then I (energetically) stormed out of the proverbial room.

The next morning, the first email in my inbox was a notification that I had won the psychic reading. I had entered nearly five months ago, and now it was time.

I yelled into the void, and it was not empty.

Did angels acknowledge my tantrum and throw me a bone? Or was this a coincidence?

If a coincidence, then what is a coincidence, exactly?

The Oxford Dictionary defines it as "a remarkable concurrence of events or circumstances without apparent causal connection."

So, is it just our brains identifying two seemingly related events and attaching more meaning to them? If so, why would our brains work that hard if not to point us to something beyond our consciousness?

Let's suppose I was yelling into the void of my psyche and only my brain heard my internal rant. Only I knew of my desire for clear spiritual communication, and winning the psychic reading was unrelated to that desire.

Yet even this does not negate the fact that the timing was beneficial to me. Even if there was no external being causing anything to happen, I benefited from the proximity of these two moments: I felt heard and seen. Without any cause, something happened when I needed it to happen.

Maybe there are no angels, no spirits, and no unseen elements of reality. If this is so, another explanation is that my subconscious brain cataloged my thought patterns and manifested them into my physical reality.

Any way you want to analyze this, even from the driest, most rational approach, there's some kind of magic happening. The way we are made, the complexities of our neural pathways, are extraordinary.

Let's continue with another example.

I have long contemplated the idea of the continued existence of souls and the ability to connect with those whose physical bodies have passed.

I have always believed that death is more a transition than an ending (although it certainly is an ending of the physical body). So, the possibility of communicating with ancestors wasn't far-fetched for me.

One day, I decided to ask my grandfather, who passed away nearly eleven years ago, a question. I needed a sign and wanted it to be unmistakable. I asked for a yes or no answer: if "yes," I wanted to see my grandmother's name; if "no," I wanted to see his name. Both had rather old-fashioned names, making random encounters unlikely.

I put in my request, then went about doing chores and clearing space, finding items to donate or sell. I went upstairs and set my focus on cleaning out a small collection of books that I had not touched in years.

The first book I pulled out was a small hardback with a blank spine and cover. When I opened it, the first page had my grandfather's full name. First, middle, last. I was shown not only his name but also his book.

The message was undeniable in its clarity.

Now, this book had been set on a shelf, likely by me. Although I had no conscious recollection of it, I must have seen it at some point. Rather than communication from my grandfather, could this have been my subconscious brain working?

Maybe I knew, without knowing I knew, that this book was there and that I could receive a "sign" if I asked for his name because I already knew I would find it. I was subconsciously giving myself an answer, my brain working with lightning speed to unpack memories and arrange a series of decisions that would lead me to where I shelved that book.

Possible, and still completely powerful.

For a moment, let's put aside the fact that consciousness itself eludes explanation and definition. Science can't tell us how our consciousness works or even what it is. Now think: if our subconscious brains can guide us *that* precisely, just think of the potential when it comes to manifestation.

My point is, *it's all magic.*

Aligned timing, gifts from spirit guides, communication with dead relatives, or sophisticated subconscious filing systems, *it's all magic.*

And we don't need to know *why* or *what*, precisely. Wonder is perhaps the most powerful emotion because it is infinitely expansive, rather than contractive. I'm becoming more comfortable sitting with *un*knowingness because that's where true expansion happens.

In the moments when the ordinary reveals itself as extraordinary, when we sit with Being and lean into the magic of the unknown, we are reminded that there is more to existence than can be captured by logic or reason.

So, as we go through life, may we remain open to the inexplicable and embrace the magic in the unknown parts that surround us, acknowledging that there is always more to discover.

In the space of the unknown lies infinite possibilities.

ABOUT MADIA SMITH

Madia is a skeptical spiritualist, fiction writer, photographer, human design enthusiast, and advocate for dumped domestic waterfowl. Once a die-hard city girl and world traveler addicted to the buzz of human movement, she suddenly found herself enjoying the starry skies in the high desert of the four corners region. Unwittingly becoming an orchardess, goose girl, and finally a mother, she is relearning the art of wonderment through close connection with the land, animals, and her brilliant husband and son.

***Instagram:** www.instagram.com/hoofandfeatherco*

7
MBK

PINK BOW UNDONE

The pink bow is undone. Tearing off the tightly taped-crumpled wrapping paper covering this package of familial disconnect. The ripping away of complicated dynamics between my two mothers and my three daughters. No Hallmark holidays for me. I am the black sheep of my family. Blah, Blah Black Sheep, share your tale.

I was twenty-one years old when I met my first blood relative. July 30, 1985, I gave birth to this magical lil being Stefanie Ann. I remember the awe and unfamiliarity I felt when my newborn baby was placed in a hospital drawer-style bassinet that I slid open, "Hello lil darling one, do you need a fresh diaper?" Fumbling with the miniature disposable diaper I changed my precious daughter for the first time.

Everything about her astounded me. I dedicated myself to raising her.

Stefanie's father, my husband, played out his family imprinting and dove even deeper into his work. Just like his father, seventy-hour work weeks were an excuse for not fully engaging with his wife and children.

I was lonely, there was no one to support me in motherhood. My mother had delayed brain surgery to be present at the birth of her first granddaughter. Shortly after Stefanie's birth, my mother had a shunt installed in her head to have the chemo more aggressively attack the latest cancer emergence.

When my mother passed away on December 10, 1985, my father looked like he was going to give up too. Ashen, I carried him about, along with my 6-month-old baby in her infant carrier. My devastated father was like a grief-stricken child, following my directions, grateful for my care.

As an antidote for his grief, my father convinced himself that he fell in love with a family friend who had also lost her long-time spouse to cancer. Six months after my mother died, my father 73 secretly eloped with his 78 yr. old bride.

I lost my father and my mother within six months. My dad with his new autocratic German wife began to act like a distant grandfather. Devastating. My inner emotional life imploding in sheer lack of nurturance.

My real mother is the woman who loved me all my life, picking me up at the hospital when my parents got the call, your baby is born! Adoption is pre-arranged by the Catholic church.

When your parents love you, even through your moody teenage years, that qualifies them as your real parents.

I always knew I was adopted, my parents said they knew nothing about my biological parents. Surprise! They knew but kept it from me because my DNA was less than flattering, dubious in character, oh let us not mince words, *trailer trash.*

I learned in my adulthood my biological mom was like a bad cat mom. Dropping a kitten here and there to be raised by whomever. I was the #6 child of an overall litter of 10 over 18 years of childbearing neglect. Too bad there isn't a trap, neuter, release program for irresponsible humans.

I was the only baby in my sketchy birth family given up for adoption.

Everyone else was just abandoned. When I met my birth family I wondered how the hell I didn't make the cut in that family.

My baby sister Christy Ann, child #10 told me, you have no idea how lucky you are, it has been hell! When I met my oldest sister Ricky Diane I began to wonder if my first name Marianne, was given to me by my adoptive parents or my biological parents.

ENOUGH WITH THE MAUDLIN TALES, LET US GET TO THE MAGIC

I was blessed abundantly to become the mother of three daughters that I adore. I was blessed to focus on each daughter, not having to leave them in daycare. I was determined to be their primary nurturer, fiercely loving and protective. If one does the math, from the time I was 21 until I was 48, I was raising children.

We had planned to have our children three years apart, but we had to work entirely too hard for our second child. I am not sure if it was truly infertility issues. When the fertility doctor learned we had sex once a week and we were in our mid-twenties he asked my husband, you are young what is up?

Louis rationalized that working 70 hours a week made once a week a good average. Truth is, I think intimacy repelled him. He told me he would prefer a back scratch to sex. Meanwhile, I had a very healthy libido, and being inexperienced, I thought my husband's lack of desire was a clear indication that I was not desirable. All three of our daughters were each born six years apart.

Wait a minute, is that the sound of a violin? Absolutely NOT.

November 1990 we got the blessed news that we were pregnant with our second child. While gestating, at 7 months pregnant, in May 1991 I stumbled upon my dutiful Catholic husband in flagrant delicato with a 17 yr. old employee.

Being 7 months pregnant I could neither kick his ass or kick her ass or get drunk.

He begged me to come home. I asked him, "What home do I have to go to?"

We went into crisis counseling. We were both still very much in love and our family was how we defined ourselves in life. I wasn't ready to give up on the dream of happily ever after. I decided not to blow up our family over one transgression.

Husbands cheating on their wives seemed commonplace. Something to grow past. It upended any sense of family or security that I previously possessed.

He promised to never work the same shift as that girl employee. Two weeks before I gave birth I found out he broke that promise as well. She had a colorful history of sleeping with management. I wonder if she kept a scorecard of her conquests.

Our second baby went ten days past her due date. She was born on July 15, 1991. I had the experience of giving birth in the water to a magical being, Chantelle Brianne. As I lifted her from the water to my chest she looked at me with these enormous, luminous blue eyes and I cooed to her, Hi! Hi! She mouthed my words, I know that sounds impossible, we have it on video.

The sound of my voice at that moment was strong, welcoming, true!

I BELIEVE I GAVE BIRTH TO A DIFFERENT VERSION OF MYSELF THAT DAY

I recognized in my being, I would never be able to count on my husband.

We had a movie set marriage but if one merely looked behind the set one would learn, it is a stage. Contrivance rampant. Connection lacking.

Bad lines and commitments, what to leave in, what to leave out.

Oh wait, those are Bob Seger lyrics but ever so apropos.

Both he & I were devout Catholics. My Catholic brain could not conceive that we would not live happily ever after. Family was everything.

Perhaps it was my hormones, perhaps it was the adultery, perhaps it was my own personal revolution brewing... approaching my thirtieth birthday cataclysmic shifts shook my foundation.

I had waist-length blonde hair, I went to my stylist and declared, "Cut a foot off and dye it red." I also broke the paradigm that if I didn't do theatre in college it was too late. I started off performing in large musicals with Inland Valley Repertory Theatre in Claremont California. Then improvisational comedy, trained by the very best, Second City Alumni.

I broke into stand-up in the Los Angeles comedy scene. Intrepidly determined, there was no reason this mother from the suburbs would be successful. Improbably within a year I had a weekly show at The Improv Comedy Club and developed their comedy school. My work has been featured in the Los Angeles Times. This professional trajectory is unheard of in stand-up comedy. Comedians are still learning to craft truly unique comedy material with a strong point of view well past their first 500 performances.

In my first year in stand-up, I was given the keys to the comedy club. Comedians are not known to walk a straight line. I had earned the reputation and recognition of being an astute businesswoman and bold performer.

I believe stand-up comedy made me a better person. It forced me to tell the truth, be present, and become more succinct and relatable. I had to stop hiding if I wanted the audience to buy what I was selling. No longer would I communicate from the place of who I thought I was supposed to be. Now it was time to speak from a place of becoming. That was when the audience began to fall in love with me, in comedian speak, this is when I became truly funny. Telling the unvarnished truth about my life. Something many people never get around to... that is what separates comedians from general citizens. Naming the elephant in the room.

With great unfoldments come new realizations and new lessons.

I admit I was a lil smug having had my two daughters before the age of thirty, my comedy career was soaring. The universe does not like smugness, time for a smackdown smarty-pants!

While on an international corporate trip with my husband in April 1997, NYC to London on the Concorde, then over to Amsterdam where we stayed at the Amstel.

He and I were virtual strangers to one another, congenial and disinterested.

He played Gin Rummy, I tore it up in fascinating Amsterdam. I led many of the other bored corporate wives astray. Coming back to the hotel just before sunrise, rattling the front doors until the sleepy hotel clerk let us cadre of naughty corporate wives back into the exclusive hotel.

On this upscale corporate vacation, my husband and I had our way with one another ONE time. It wasn't even notable.

I arrived home to find out inconceivably, but ever so conceivably, I was pregnant for a third time!

Good God, no need for infertility treatment this time. Pregnant despite endometriosis and fibroid tumors. This baby was determined to join our family. I cried for nine months and then

January 21, 1998, I gave birth to a 9.5 lb. magical being who would not be denied,

Monet Lillana. One of the biggest blessings of my life.

My husband and I lived separate lives. I was a mommy by day, a comedian by night.

This was my Aphrodite decade, and I no longer was interested in playing by the rules.

Love had proven to be an enormous disappointment. My husband had no idea how to love me. Truth be told, I had no idea how to love me.

Love got me wounded. Left me bleeding and broken on the floor of my rock bottom. I did not need further entanglements or enmeshment.

Shortly before I turned forty I decided to slip off the golden handcuffs of my empty, privileged marriage. It was my sincere desire to model a healthier way of living, instead of settling for broken promises and Catholic subterfuge. This was the modus operandi of my former husband's family.

I didn't end my marriage for some partner waiting in the wings. I ended my marriage because I did not want to spend my life not knowing what it was to be loved. I thought I married the wrong person. I thought finding the right person, I would experience what it is to be wholeheartedly loved.

I tried so hard to mitigate the collateral damage of divorce that *I became the collateral damage.*

My two older daughters decided to not allow me to be a part of their children's lives.

I suspect it will be a slow dawning for my daughters on the tremendous personal cost of erasing their mother for decades. They chose to simply not deal with their emotional issues.

A trait learned from their father's family.

My former husband's heart literally blew from all the things he did not want to acknowledge or feel. He died at the all too-young age of 53 from a massive heart attack. Tragic.

Despite their father's sudden death, my daughters continue to ignore my existence. My daughters will one day realize the price for denying the fabric from which they were rendered. I know in my being that we are cut of the same cloth.

My oldest daughter has a tattoo on her inner forearm, Daddy's Little Disappointment. That is between the two of them. I never spoke ill of their father, even when he was doing his best to destroy me. Honestly, he came close. There were times I was so low I thought about how to exit.

My youngest daughter, Monet, suffered greatly as well. I tried to protect her but the vindictiveness of my former husband and our two older daughters' complicity was formidable, difficult to pin down. Accountability slid off them.

At 17, my middle daughter's reward for leaving my home without my permission, Chantelle received a brand-new car, a faux adulthood, and a credit card to furnish her father's new hilltop home. Incredible view, zero perspective.

Her father enrolled Chantelle in a plot to take custody of my youngest daughter, allegedly so the sisters could be together. Three terrifying years in family law court and my former husband did not get anything he asked for and was ordered to pay me even more support. He could have kept his shekels, I would have preferred we focused on parenting our daughters without rancor. I did not grow up in a family where the father undercut the mother. Sadly, that is how his family of origin operated. Lots of repression, lies, and secrets. I don't pop with that.

My two older daughters chose to side with their father and ice me out of their lives. I understand that it was lucrative and much easier than being held accountable by their highly intuitive mother.

My oldest daughter literally told me, "Mom be very clear, when Chantelle and I choose not to be in a relationship with you, it is because to be in a relationship with you, requires us to be accountable to ourselves."

Sorry darlin, that one is a non-negotiable.

I am grateful I chose to escape a patriarchal toxic family system and modeled what it is to live as a fully expressed woman. Perfectly imperfect. I modeled this to my daughters, and I lived into it for myself.

In the words of Anne Lamott: *The greatest gift we can give our children is healing ourselves.*

I hold each of my daughters in LOVE. Recognizing their complete ostracizing of me, although incredibly painful, was the alchemizing force of me becoming all that I am. No pink bows attached to this package.

Through these painful years of estrangement, I have reached out and received the silent treatment on full mute.

I have learned I cannot force a solution, that mothers are not as important as I thought they were, and that my fierce love for my daughters seems to account for very little.

Lest you think we have tipped over into the darkness I bring to you the focused magic.

In 2020 I left Southern California where I had spent the first fifty-five years of my life.

Sold my house of 30 years, gave away most of what I owned, and drove into the discovery of a new life.

Me and my two dogs, and an F150 truck loaded with my remaining belongings rolled into Mancos, Colorado on July 4, 2020. We stayed one night at the very nice Starry Nights BnB.

I agonized over how I would ever find and establish our new home. I knew no one in Southwest Colorado. Little did I know the ancestors called us here to this healing, sacred land.

My ancestors were probably amused at my inner lamenting about where would we go, and how would we find home. Lo and behold, I bought my dream ranch right next door to Starry Nights.

The very place I arrived.

I have created Story Tree Guest Ranch. I have over 30 four-legged healers on staff. I have filled the ranch one precious animal at a time. Creating my beloved animal family. Each animal has a unique story. Horses, llamas, a donkey, a pig, many goats & sheep, chickens, ducks, dogs, and a barn cat.

I experience tremendous, unadulterated love from each of these animals. I am healed in their pure love. The sense of peace I get caring for them is immeasurable and ever-present.

Despite my life going sideways, including my long-term marriage ending, my two older daughters choosing their father exclusively, deliberately erasing me from their lives.

Loved ones followed the money and wrote off their perceived losses, namely me.

I THOUGHT FAMILY WAS THE MOST IMPORTANT THING IN LIFE

Maybe learning to love oneself is the most important principle to live into.

I have so much more compassion and understanding for myself, for my former husband, and for my daughters. Maybe we have played our prescribed roles perfectly, in this lifetime.

Formerly, I was the irritant, stirring up people's demons. Life has bludgeoned me into a better version of myself. The sharp edges of my hubris knocked off.

I have found peace. I have found love. It is within me. It is what I am made of. It is my purpose. My identity. My expression.

What does a life lived less ordinary look like?

I host a guest ranch dedicated to animal lovers.

I produce and direct original theatre, for over 30 years, cultivating empowered communicators and deep listeners through the Theatre Arts.

I am an internationally performing comedian, writer & storyteller, I delight in sharing stories of life's lessons with aplomb.

Here I am in the present, no pink bow, no Hallmark moments.

In deep gratitude for the alchemy of love.

Focused magic indeed. -MBK

ABOUT MBK

MBK is a writer, producer, and director of original theatre for the past 30 years. She is passionate about cultivating empowered communication and deep listening. An internationally performing stand-up comedian who has performed throughout New York City, Chicago, Seattle, Los Angeles, Sydney, Australia and Queenstown, New Zealand. She taught performance at The Improv Comedy Club and her work has been featured in the Los Angeles Times. MBK is an accomplished storyteller who has performed with The Moth, Story District in Washington DC, and at the legendary Esalen in Big Sur, California.

She has realized a lifelong dream of creating a guest ranch for people who love animals & stories. Story Tree Ranch - Tales & Tails a plenty. With over 30 animal healers on staff, guests bask in the beauty of Southwest Colorado, a mere 15 minutes from Mesa Verde National Park. Guests also revel in the pure love and presence of friendly horses, llamas, a donkey, goats, sheep, ducks, dogs, chickens, a barn cat, and a highly verbal, free-range pig named Charlotte. MBK is currently Artistic Director of Bridging Stories, an Intergenerational Story Sharing Program that partners students & elders. Developing empowered communicators and skilled listeners, in the Art of Story Sharing. She is also mother to three amazing women and Grandmama to six grandchildren. MBK has embodied a life lived less ordinary, a love of world travel and everyday adventure.

Website: *www.ConspireToInspire.us*

8
MEG ASHLEY KORF-MORALES

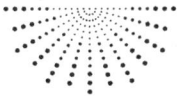

GUT FEELINGS

A year ago, I embarked on a journey within a journey, not quite aware of the magic that was going to unfold.

I began my recovery journey many years ago, with failed attempts in between, but made the final commitment to myself last February and put down alcohol once and for all. This isn't just the same, uplifting sobriety or recovery story that you've heard a million times. My recovery journey just happens to be interwoven into the journey I want to share about here: finding Meg.

Ten days after I had decided that I could no longer live the lifestyle I was, my cousin, whom I considered an older sister at the time, called me exclaiming she had a proposition for my husband and me, and that this proposition would benefit all of us in the long run. In a custody battle for her two older children from a previous marriage, a toddler and a new baby from her present and tumultuous marriage, she was overwhelmed and needed help. Her husband, an extremely successful business owner, and absolute lunatic, had bought a multi-million dollar, 23-acre property in Mancos, Colorado that just so happens to have a brand-new apartment on it, completely separate from the house. My cousin's offer to us was if I cleaned their house five days a week, and my husband maintains the outside of the property, we could live in the apartment as a trade for work.

At the time, I was newly sober, and feeling stuck back in my hometown, so I took this opportunity seriously into consideration...it sounded almost too good to be true but perhaps it could also be the change we needed.

There was an intense energy of pressure and urgency to make a decision of my cousin's offer. She didn't give us this offer and said, "Take your time thinking about it, I know it's a big move." She was desperate for help (and a friend), and somehow believed us being there would solve a lot of her problems.

My cousin had been unhappy in her marriage for quite some time. She married a man, much older than her, who was seemingly not who he said he was. As a wealthy businessman, with hundreds of employees and projects to manage, he never made enough time for my cousin and their two, young kids and controlled all the money. I had only met him once at their wedding, and he was a pretty bland guy who is into a lot of off-putting conspiracy theories and is constantly working on what he considers spirituality and enlightenment. I mean it when I tell you this guy has a very dark, evil energy about him, so I didn't blame her for wanting out of their marriage. It turned out that he had shot the neighbor's dog shortly before we arrived, which was kept from me in her fear of us changing our mind.

I really believed my cousin was giving us full transparency on the situation. She wanted help around the house so she could have more quality time to spend with their kids, figure out custody with her two older kids from her previous marriage, and eventually make a plan to leave her husband. According to her, this plan was nowhere in the future and we would have plenty of time to settle down before any big decisions were made.

We began making plans to move around the end of April or the beginning of May (2023). That gave us 3 months to sell all of our things, and put tangible steps into place. We were made promises like they would be absolutely flexible with days/amount of hours needed in the house and on the property once we got jobs. Our main goal was to own our property someday, not be controlled by anyone else, so we knew we wanted to get jobs as soon as we got out here to start saving money. That was just fine by them and we were all able to compromise and meet in the middle. They ensured we would not be taken advantage of and vice versa. After multiple, open and (what we thought were) honest conversations over the phone with them, we came to an agreement that we all felt comfortable with. However, as the day to move got closer, they began to implement changes that should've been obvious red flags, but I chalked the awful feeling in my gut to nerves and fear of venturing away from my family and didn't allow myself to go more deeply with how I felt.

We started selling and giving away all of our things that wouldn't fit in the trunk of my 2008 Honda Accord, Big Betsy. It was going to be my dad, my husband, our (then) two-year-old daughter, and our 10-year-old dog in the car, so space was limited. Since we officially made the decision to take an opportunity that would better our lives, we now had about two and a half months to move out of our studio cabin, sell my husband's car and tools, get Big Betsy tuned up, and have enough money saved for everything we would need for this trip and our new apartment. Four or five weeks out from our planned departure date, my cousin called me and said that her husband had decided that they needed to collect a $2,000 security deposit for the apartment since it was brand new, and needed the back-up insurance in case we damaged it in any way.

In addition to that, rent was equivalent to $2,400, and they wanted to make rent equal to a certain number of hours worked per month, instead of a dollar amount. I was expected to clean the house 5 days a week, with specific tasks and "projects" assigned to each day/week/month. I am not a cleaner nor is housekeeping what I wanted to do with my life, but it sounded reasonable and like something I could manage temporarily, to better my family's life in the long run. Still, something about that last minute adjustment didn't sit right with me and that awful feeling in my gut immediately surfaced. But once again, I concluded it was just nerves and even though this feeling got worse the closer the day got, and I could not stop crying a whole week beforehand, we stuck with our plans to come out to Colorado.

On May 14th, 2023, we said our very painful goodbyes to our family and embarked on this new journey. We took 3 days to enjoy the trip with my dad and made sure to stop at all the places where our hearts felt called to.

On the second day of our trip, 20 miles away from our destination for the night, my (recently tuned-up) car's alternator died, putting us about half a day behind. I immediately suspected this was a sign from the universe that I may have made the wrong decision and doomed my family. Was it too late to turn back now? I quickly redirected my thinking to it was only a setback, and we were able to get my car into a mechanic and on the road by the next afternoon.

After three, long, emotional days had passed, we had finally arrived at my cousin and her husband's property. We made it! We were here and we were ready to start a new chapter of our lives. My dad stayed for a couple more days to help us settle in and check out the area, and then he was gone. That was a really, really tough day.

Our first week was a week of settling in and getting out in the community. As a woman who thrives on socializing and connecting with other human beings, I knew that in order to stay positive, I had to explore the four corners and meet new people. We weren't expected to start working on the property until the following week, so we took advantage of our free time. Prior to moving, we enrolled our daughter at the local preschool in Mancos and they were holding a fundraiser at the local brewery. I dressed up and the 3 of us went down, met a diversity of humans, bid on some silent auction items, had a fabulous pizza, and for the first time since deciding to do this, I took a deep belly breath. Okay, I thought, I didn't totally screw up my family's life. It was going to be okay. We were going to be okay.

I ended up getting a job bartending at the brewery a week later. It came with its challenges being only 4 months sober at the time, but it got me out of the house and into the community, and I was making money to boot. I slowly started opening myself up and began making invaluable connections and a few life-long friends, who started out as coworkers.

On the other hand, we were miserable working for my cousin and her husband. As soon as I began working at the brewery and making friends, my cousin completely changed. Not only did she not adjust my days/hours once I got a job, but she also started adding chores and projects. It seemed like the happier and more comfortable I got within the community, the more I had to do for her. I cleaned their massive kitchen including the dining room, living room, bedrooms, kids' bedrooms, bathrooms (all 5 of them), ALL of their laundry, and the list would just get bigger or more in-depth. If I accidentally missed something, I would receive passive-aggressive text messages with pictures attached, saying I needed to come back and finish the job...even if I had to go to work in the next hour.

My husband's side of the agreement also began changing, and 25-30 hours a month turned into a mandatory 25 hours a week. With the dollar amount of rent and new adjustments to their agreement, it came out to my husband working for $10 an hour. When I brought this up to my cousin, because it was really starting to feel like we were getting taken advantage of, she said that was why they wanted rent to be set up that way. I explained to her that it seemed shady, and she responded, "Yeah, I don't know what to say."

At this point, I am thinking to myself, "What in the actual fuck have I gotten my family and myself into." My husband is working his ass off for pennies on the dollar, not to mention him having to accompany my cousin's husband every other week on a 6-hour drive to Bailey, Colorado and back, to help them get their house there completely cleaned out and ready to put on the market. I am missing my family so terribly by now, my heart is constantly heavy with a mixture of guilt, homesickness, and regret. The only light I experience at this time is the connections I've made through the brewery, and our days off from working, to get out and explore everything that Southwest Colorado has to offer.

The more time I spend with my cousin, the more tension that develops in our relationship. I am waking up irritated, already dreading the next four hours ahead of me, and never knowing what to expect at this point, even a month later. That awful feeling in my gut comes back with vengeance, and I'm not sure what's coming, but it doesn't feel good.

One week later, five short weeks after uprooting our lives as we knew them, that awful gut feeling was rightfully justified. My cousin was making an escape plan to leave her husband, take their two kids, and go down to Georgia to stay with her mom, all while he was up in Bailey, packing up the last of their house. What struck us the most - all of this was going down in 6 days. After the pure disbelief and undeniable feeling of being betrayed wore off, I tried empathy. My cousin was miserable in her marriage, and in the back of my mind, I had known it was always a possibility that things would not work out in some form or another. I am a being of positive energy, love and light and to find hope or magic in times where it seems nonexistent feels damn near impossible. I used to say everything happens for a reason, because goddammit I believed it, but then I read this: Some things are just really, really shitty and they should never have happened. And there is a strange sense of hope in that. We don't have to make sense of everything or try to find some grand meaning behind it. But there was a lesson in this.

My husband and I were frantically discussing what our next steps were going to entail- should we move back home to California? It has only been five weeks, we've barely given ourselves a chance to make it here. Should we stay? If we do, how can we possibly find a place to rent in 6 days? We have to give it our best shot, we can always go back home if it doesn't pan out.

So, we stay. I was able to put all of my hurt aside, put my head on straight, and find us an apartment to rent in the nearby town. Luckily, I had a job at the brewery, and we had enough money to secure our apartment. The next 6 days were a blur and I've suppressed a lot of it until now. My cousin and I got into a hurtful fight over text messages, where she said we should be grateful for her kindness, and we should've had a plan B as we are adults. We never really resolved it, just played nice to get through the next 5 days and all of this chaos was over.

We pretended like nothing was happening around her husband and prayed that he wouldn't catch on. The day to leave came as fast as it went. My cousin drove right by us, with no apology, well wishes, or goodbyes. She never reached out to us and to this day, I still have not heard from her. That's what truly hurts the most.

I was devastated for a long time and even worse, I was drowning in guilt. I felt betrayed, alone, and I began resenting my job at the brewery. I could hardly bear the weight of regret for uprooting my husband and daughter's lives for something I felt so sure of.

After feeling sorry for myself for months, I decided enough is enough. We are here and there has to be more to this story than the utter defeat presently swallowing me.

We will live close to my family again, but for right now, I need to embrace the beauty and opportunities all around us. I had to take a deep look inside of my soul and ask if I wanted to stay stuck, when I'll be stuck either way, or do I want to find out what parts of me are meant to grow and heal here. I choose to grow and heal. Let what is meant to find me, find me in passion and kindness and hope.

Not long after I took on this powerful new mindset, I quit the brewery. As a person in recovery, I no longer felt like bartending aligned with my journey, and I had gotten everything I needed from my experiences there. I will forever be grateful for the friendships and support I found at the brewery when I had no one else.

The magic of manifestation is truly out there, we just have to believe and call it in, day after day until it has made a home in our minds.

For the first time in my life, I can feel in my spirit that I am on my true path. The previous paths I've traveled are just one small fraction of the whole journey.

I have found the beauty and importance of connecting with other women, whether it be recovery support groups or women who have done exactly what you want to do- that is achieve their highest self no matter what odds were against them.

I have found myself more inspired here than I have ever been before in my life, and I have found purpose in all the madness, disappointment, and heartbreak.

I am meant to be here now to learn and connect with powerful beings, and to be shown by women who are living proof, that if you focus on the magic, and ignore anyone who doesn't believe in your magic, you can be exactly who you were meant to be and do exactly what you were meant to do.

I discovered parts of myself on this journey that I didn't know were so strong and I discovered parts of myself on this journey that I didn't know were so soft. I discovered that not all family will be there for you, and some might even completely fuck you over, but you know what? You meet people who have just as much shit going on as you and you connect with them, and you laugh and you cry, and you wake up one day and realize a piece of your spirit is starting to heal. And the weights you've born for too long, lift off of you and disappear into a lifetime ago, as if they were never yours to bear in the first place.

As I continue to heal and grow, I know someday I will find forgiveness in my heart, in order to heal this part of me too. Writing about it was the first step. For the rest of this journey, I am going to be present. I'm going to keep healing those raw parts of my spirit and I am going to give myself grace as I do so.

I am magic.

ABOUT MEG ASHLEY KORF-MORALES

Meg Morales is a California transplant in Southwest Colorado. She is a woman in recovery and is a huge supporter and advocate for recovery. Meg has an unstoppable passion for helping other women in or seeking recovery and serves as a Certified Professional for the She Recovers Foundation. Meg is also a trained end-of-life doula, with a focus on grief support for substance use and addiction-related deaths, and has been pursuing her degree in Psychology as well. She loves nature and belongs to the ocean. She currently lives near the Four Corners with her husband, daughter, Goose the dog, and two cats, Douglas and Zelda.

Facebook: www.facebook.com/profile.php?id=61557722366145&mibextid=ZbWKwL
Instagram: www.instagram.com/thelovedlife_

9
RHED LEONARD

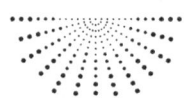

STATUS QUO, A DANGEROUS PLACE TO STAY

We are all born knowing magic, feeling magic, breathing, and living our own special magic.

I knew about magic when I was young, that the air was magic. I could fly, could soar in my dreams and in big loud airplanes and in shiny sleek spaceships. I could float words like scintillating kites in the air and touch all the other magical selves with them.

Water was magic! I could skim and shiver through it, swimming, making keen wakes in the river of life, sliding smooth from rock to rock, not quite touching the earth. I knew water was my blood and my soft heart and my taste for salt and the color blue. I loved water the most: it felt like freedom and a comforting hug all at once; Mother safety for me to learn to be a magical human within.

Earth magic called me to quest with elves and dwarves and living trees for dragons and trolls and to vanquish sorcerers. Earth called me to sit under giant trees, make magnificent mud pies, and dig for gold in the dirt and in my child heart. Earth is where the soul of the planet resides, where she keeps us in secret and restores us for the next go around as beings of soil and eating.

She eats us, we eat her, as a child I was born knowing this. I never doubted I would eat well and be a good dessert in my time.

Fire is magical; it is the power to lead one both through and abruptly out of childhood. Those wee lights we follow willy nilly towards our dreams and our heart's desires, they do lead us to quest. They stay ahead of us and our glad-reaching little hands as long as they can. That fire warms us when we don't know we need it, baking spiritual cookies to slow us down, to entice us to remain children just a little longer. Then, when we finally catch up to those sparks and sprites, they show us the magic of transformation from infant to sentient being, and that is where there is a chink to drive a wedge into.

Being born hurts, every time.

In this time when we are most open to change, we are changed. Our new sentience asks why. This never hurt before, why now? Why can't I fly or swim or dig or...why does fire hurt so much this time?

Poor burned Humanity has resisted the transformative fire of learning to see beyond ourselves, and has embraced the idea that we must run run run away from the fire that made us sentient in the first place.

In the interest of running from all our born wisdom, we are taught by those fleeing life's great and perfect kiln that magic is Santa Claus, or Baba Yaga, or silly chants or turning lead into gold or balls of plasma shooting from the palms of some dastardly sage, or evil witches flying on broom giving out warts or souring the milk of their neighbor's cows or demons or even the Devil...all things our child hearts know are not real. They try to make us fear magic at the same time they try to make us forget that magic is us.

We are taught at the earliest age they can insert the message, that magic is a belief, an opinion... a falsehood. That "belief" in "magic" is nothing more than ridiculous regression back to the infancy of humanity.

Now inherently terrified of pain and change, we vigorously program our young, not even always just teaching, that magic is not in the knowing, but in the believing. Belief is malleable, changeable...belief takes us from knowing to wondering, always wondering. That arbitrary removal of true knowledge makes life taste bitter and feel pointless. But we've been successfully sold the belief that we can't change anything, because trying only leads to getting burned.

We've long long long-ago lost sight of the beauty of transformation. Imagine never letting a caterpillar learn it could be a butterfly if you'd just quit breaking open the cocoon to save it from turning to go first.

We are encouraged to swallow the rotten taste of a life that is dull, fixed in place and without purpose or even forward motion, as a person or a species. All in the interest of a collective refusal to change, generationally rooted and normalized. We have stripped ourselves of the thing that will keep us from self-destructing in our youth as a species.

We know in the center of us, near our connection with the womb, perhaps, that the magic is there, but we can't see it anymore. We're gaslit into believing that only children believe in magic, and thereby convinced that being children somehow makes us wrong.

In convincing us that magic is a belief and not a knowing, they cover up the magic in us, they gouge out our infant mind's eye, so we won't see it anymore.

When we question that magic isn't and can't be a known thing, because it is just a silly belief, we are burned, not for the sake of growing, like sequoias are burned to make them shed seed, or a Japanese sword is heated and pounded into something ruthlessly beautiful, no nothing so valiant or worthy: we are burned to trigger the pain of becoming, without the assurance that the pain will pass and we will be new again. We are burned in our hearts by fearful elders, bitter generations of the gaslit who came before us, burned to show us that we must avoid the bigger fire.

The fire is magic, and it brings CHANGE. Magic is change. To have magic power is the power to make change, to grow, and become something you weren't before. Magic is the power to give birth, to more of us, to ideas that can make the world better for us all.

But change hurts. The burning pain of transformation gives a choice to become or stay the same. Our collective has decided no amount of beatification and ascension is worth any amount of discomfort. We are stuck as self-centered youth. With the chrysalis cracked so early on, there are few if any butterflies among us now. Sadly, it's to the point where our collective 'knows" there never were any, that that is the stuff of ridiculous magical fairy tales.

We still have magic though. You cannot be alive in this Universe without magic. We can't see it anymore, but we kill and rape and starve and bomb and hate and destroy our planet with it. We allow the destruction to flow because we've gaslit countless generations that it can't be us because we don't have that power.

I am thankful that we are part and parcel of the Universe regardless, because that means we can't destroy the whole thing on our own. It's so big, we are just dust. The magic of being is bigger than us. That's why we are all born knowing magic and the gaslighting must be repeated with each generation. We keep trying to grow that infant eye back.

It's an impossible life task to make art for the blind, but those of us whose eyes have budded, must. We must outgrow the gnawing fear the dead possess, the fear of those who chose not to embrace the magic of change. We must outgrow the fear of life in all its messiness, its unexpected turns, and bittersweet glory.

We must remember there IS magic, and that magic is us. It's not a belief that we can be changed, or that we can change reality... We and only we make our changes. And we ARE making changes-and they will kill us all as surely as any burning sun. Magic wasn't banished, we are all made blind to it. We must take that knowledge back. Magic is in us, it IS us...magic is a real tangible power. It is not ridiculous cartoons and fantasies, it is what makes the sun burn, the planet spin, the oceans slosh, and the air flow. It is our choices and our actions.

FOCUS ON THE MAGIC

Magic is inherent in being, magic power is conferred upon sentience.

THE BATTLE OF NEVERWAS (HOW I ESCAPED, AND THE MAP OF THE WAY OUT)

When I was born I knew there was magic, it was all around me plain to see.
My soft baby hands could mold and ply and twist it so easily.
My tender infant heart saw through the meat to the heart of things.
That Human I was like all else, of Earth of Air and Water, and Fiery wings.
Then I was dipped in the molten void and told otherwise.

I hid because I liked the fairies and the talking to foxes.
Born wise, somehow I knew I would have wings one day.
I hid and they found me, cut me up, and put the parts in boxes.
They kept the mushy parts and used them like stinking clay.
They dipped me and shaped me to the preferred size.
Laughing in ignorance, they pulled my wings off.
"You don't need those."
Then my beautiful antennae made them scoff.
"You don't need those."
My eyes, my songs, my words my spirit, way too soft.
"You don't need those."
"You don't need those."

"We don't need those."

So, stripped of all glory and left to wander the world blind and wingless.
I laid down in what had been cool glorious pies of good black dirt.
Now only feeling muck and filth, shame and weakness: stingless.

RHED LEONARD

On my back staring up sightless at glory, feeling only hurt.
This is life they say, don't act so surprised.

I put what pieces were left together in a way that could serve.
I lurched and stumbled and strained to be.
All that was required of me, I never swerved.
I succeeded, but also failed, I failed to be me.
I failed to be whole again, and wise.

I hid, better this time, my parts regrowing till even I could feel it.
They found me, but this time instead of freezing, I fought.
They tried to make me cut out my own heart, so they could steal it.
I hid and healed and sealed up the chrysalis and sought.
To grow fast enough to outrun a second excise.

In secret, a second womb of my choice, my wings unfurled.
"Ah, how I've needed these."
In my self-made mother space, my antennae uncurled.
"Ah, how I've needed these."
My eyes my songs my words my spirit all awhirl.
'Ah, how I've needed these."
'Oh, how I've needed these."

"Ahhhhhhh, how I've missed these."

So, as a re-winged being, fully hatched, I fly not unafraid but undaunted.
I search for the faint pheromonal scent of others like me.
I feel the magic of knowing again, and I'm not haunted.
No more fear of change, change is what made you and me.
You can re-wing too, be not afraid to rise.

Own yourself, own your magic, own your place in this Universe.
Your second wings can be those of powerful dragons.

Or butterflies, or night birds, or winged fish...what could be worse.
Then letting this ancient fear drain your flagon.
And leave you empty in your own eyes?

Go ahead; you've read this much, keep looking in this mirror, the best part is coming up!

If you see any part of yourself here, it is because you are so not alone. You have been a part of the biggest mindfuckery campaign in the history of humankind. You have been convinced there is nothing to see here, that you are not an intrinsically potent being, capable of surviving the hardships that temper us into stronger beings. Message: You are weak and only useful to others, you can never be useful to yourself.

Think. Who is giving this message? It does not come from the Universe. It comes from your deluded siblings! It is a mindless reflex we all share now, with less meaning now than it had in the first place.

You have been gaslit. It's been going on for so long, it feels normal. It feels like proper tradition. It feels like history we must respect by repeating the same fuckup with every new generation. Pulling off wings is not always enough. We have crucified and burned at the stake our winged ones at every opportunity in order to preserve the conflict/scarcity mindset.

So, instead of recognizing all beings as the siblings they are, we only see competition. Instead of being reassured by the knowledge that love has no limits, we fight and squabble for our share of an unlimited resource! We go through our lives feeling helpless, in the face of our own vast power to grow and become. We let others whose worldview is rooted in this destructive cycle confuse and berate us and cause us to doubt our own connection with the Universe!

We are all suffering from this gaslighting one way or the other...I take that back: there are cultures on this planet that still live their magic, untrammeled. Some of those folk know the danger the greater world holds for them, and they have killed to defend their peace. Who can blame them?

How can we bring the magic back? We can own our part in this deluded, limiting view of ourselves. We can acknowledge that *the magic never left*, that we have given up our eye for it. We can stop pulling the wings and souls off of each other and our children. We can hold nourishing space for each other to grow those precious bits back. We CAN. If we do, Magic will be present and flowing through humanity once more.

It's happening, jump on that wagon…or break your own trail, but don't sit content with being less than you were meant for. Learn to see your magic again. Learn to live whole.

POEMS THAT MARK A HEALING JOURNEY; LET ME SHARE MY VISION

(when the cycles of repeating pain become too much)

> *Mercurial waves cross and make riptides.*
> *Unfinished past and present collide.*
> *Tearing into our tender soul-bearing meat.*
> *Rending out the black nuggets that seat*
> *themselves in us, and eat*
> *Our happiness.*
> *All the waves of time combine.*
> *All the pains of time on rewind*
> *Piercing veils, a searing gift*
> *A chance to heal the gaping rift.*
> *To close the wounds that let sift*
> *away our joy.*

FOCUS ON THE MAGIC

I hold this space for us all, and you
As we careen in the cleansing slough
Chronos dashing us, breaking crystal stain
Violent waters tossing us, giving us again
Time to relive and release pain,
And find peace.

(On taking advantage of opportunities to grow up through hardship like it's a sidewalk)

Today the Sun's face will hide
Allowing us to see what is in our darkness.

Today, as the Sun rises, I will bathe.
I will scrub my mortal flesh with salt and rosemary,
reaching into my spirit, abluting time's stale crumbs.
I will flood my hair- sacred channel to ancient fam;
I will flood my hair with rosemary and water warmed like
    my blood,
So wisdom can flow.

Today, as the sun ascends, I will prepare.
I will set the stones and the bones in a circle
beneath a mother tree, whose roots offer
an earth burrow for my spirit.

Today, as the sun goes cold, I will sit
In the protected womb of stone and bone
I will sit in the dark place with my ancient fam
And listen to our heart.

Today, when the sun emerges, so shall I
return with ancient knowing.

RHED LEONARD

Blessed be the New Moon and uncovered Sun.

(What to do for anyone who needs help growing their wings back)

Soul tired sister
You called me
Your living well is dry
If you had tears to cry
You'd drink them

Soul tired sister
I hear you!
Come to the Great Well
Where Sacred Feminine dwells
Slake your thirst

Soul tired sister
Drink with me
We will prime your spring
Ever flowing, let us bring
Your spirit back

Soul tired sister
Rest you now
The great river within you roars
Out from behind the dam, it soars
To replenish you.

Blessed be your Mind's Eye
Blessed be your Voice
Blessed be your Heart
Blessed be your Hands
Blessed be your Feet
Blessed be, and be Soul tired no more.

FOCUS ON THE MAGIC

(Excerpt from my social media, where I share all the healings. A bit of my power coming back, and what that can look like for you, too)

"I realized (was shown by spirit guides for the nth damn time) that my earning power goals were not in line with my authentic witch self/spiritual healer/self-love goals. Yes, I manifested what I wanted this last half year, with help from ancient fam...so I could see very clearly that that is not good for me, only others. I was still trying too hard to serve others. Edit: serving others is not the same as helping and healing!

I saw that those who need me have always found me. No need to put so much of my limited energy into seeking them out. I am already a magnet.

I saw that trying to be a regular Ole retailer was contaminating my dark empath gift and keeping me on a constant roller-coaster of building up pollution and sickening to purge it out. Public exposure even 3 days a week was clogging me up with increasingly random health issues.

Under these conditions, there is no way I can help myself, let alone anyone else.

So, I took a leap of faith. I DECIDED to serve my highest purpose only, no compromise involving trying to make money. I TRUSTED my ancient fam's message that the money will come if I follow my magic.

I decided to accept that I am a hermit healer, a Namer of Monsters and Pain, a Maker of Power Objects, and art of course, and a living psychopomp. And I stopped worrying about money.

Tears of joy flowing freely as I write this.

Immediately felt IT. No lightning bolt, no jump up and hallelujah, just...the light came on. Peace, equilibrium, surety...replaced the panic I had lived with my whole life.

Felt great, but a little tired, right? So, I took a nap, woke up feeling fresh and happy, and randomly decided to join Witchy Woman's Market. Posted my little candles...the next morning, less than 12 hrs later, I had sold out!!! SOLD OUT. AND 3 shops asked to carry my candles. The comments are turned off, but the post is still receiving love, from literally hundreds of people, and the number is still rising.

I am making more candles this week! Hundreds more, that are already sold. Candles are a JOY to make! Making them energizes my heart.

Ancient fam and the Divine rewards the worthy student. I will not be worrying about money anymore. And I am fully here to heal those who need me. Herbalism, ritual, holding space, Naming the dark...

Thank you ancient fam, and my beloved Brigid. Thank you, Sun and Moon for letting me see so clearly into my darkness."

(Another excerpt, very recent at this writing ...what it looks like to defend your choices once you finally find your magic and unfurl your wings in strength.)

"A while back, I posted about a fraction of some major self-knowledge downloads... soul epiphany.

I thought the rest might be too complex to express, that it might take many years to unravel.

In truth, it was that it was too simple to meet my expectations, so I spent a lot of time chewing on it.

My sacred power, purpose, and methodology have become crystal clear.

I BELIEVE IN A REAL-TIME, FULL SPECTRUM EXPERIENCE OF AND RESPONSE TO LIFE.

I choose not to impose any feelings upon myself that are not an authentic response to life as it unfolds, not to suffer or feel joy without cause.

My much sought-after and finally realized baseline is contentment. Therein lies my peace.

I will be aggressive about making sure I am not restrained or cajoled into changing this path.

I will not leave a perfectly good bushel of lemons to rot at my feet whilst pursuing an arbitrary campaign to control what should flow freely through me, within the Universe.

EVERYTHING THAT COMES TO ME FROM THE UNIVERSE IS FOR MY BENEFIT.

When the bitter fruit comes, I will make lemonade, limoncello, lemon cream pie, lemon marmalade, and very effective household cleaner. And doing so will bring me back to contentment.

I will be as grateful for bitter fruit as I am for sweet nectar. It is all meant to nourish me.

I will spend a year in mourning. (sic: my mother had just died) When I am done, I will not have wasted any precious fruit.

Strength lies in knowing your own path, and not being diverted from it once you find it."

That is how I have regained sight of my magic and yours. I have big, beautiful starship wings. They were so hard to regrow, but so worth it.

Thank all of you for witnessing my story.

ABOUT RHED LEONARD

Rhed Leonard is a multi-heritage American hedgewitch. She is on an evolving journey to help others find and heal their personal power through connecting with Nature.

Facebook: *www.facebook.com/profile.php?id=61552995697464&mibextid=ZbWKwL*

10
TINA WEFER

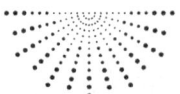

THE JOY OF SELF-DISCOVERY: EMBRACING YOUR PERSONAL MAGIC

It all started in June of 2019.

I was surrounded by whirling thoughts and questions…
"Who am I???"
"What am I doing here?"
… until something massively shifted in my life.

Like all other catalysts, this one came out of nowhere and had a profound effect on every aspect of my life as I knew it. We have all heard people talk about midlife or identity crises, and we tend to think of men buying sports cars or boats, but mine was something entirely different.

It was an awakening.

It was a rebirth found in the form of self-discovery that allowed me to finally reveal my radical authenticity, embrace my inner magic, and begin to create an entirely new reality.

It all started in June of 2019 when I found my biological sister through a DNA test.

Convincing her that I was her sister took time, as she was looking for a sister born on a different day and with a different name, and although I was born in the city she expected and my birthdate was close, she remained uncertain.

The site suggested we were half-sisters, and I tried to convince her that DNA doesn't lie. Despite providing the facts, she was focused on finding her sister Susan, born on Susan's birthdate.

We spent the day messaging back and forth, with her asking questions and me trying to provide convincing answers, and I anxiously awaited each notification of a new message. Finally, she looked up my Facebook account and, after seeing how similar I look to our mother, she was convinced.

Finding my biological family gave me so much information I'd wanted my entire life.

Is my red hair hereditary?

What's in my health history?

Is my melanoma hereditary or do I need to be a hermit the rest of my life?

Who are these people and what are they like?

How did I come to be in this world?

Do I have siblings?

I knew that my adoptive family cherished me, but I had always had so many questions.

As grateful as I was for answers, along with the answers came more questions.

Not only had my name and birthdate been changed, but I had also created stories about who my parents were, how they'd met, and how I'd come to be in the world.

Of course, none of the stories were true, because they were based on a little girl's imagination.

I felt torn between the person I'd been for 49 years and the information that I learned from finally finding my biological family. It felt like I was two different people that I was trying to reconcile.

How did this change me?

Who am I and who do I want to be?

I had enjoyed my life before having this new information. I enjoyed the clients I worked with and the products I built. I had a partner, good friends, and traveled. I wanted for nothing... except true happiness.

See, as a child, I had what I needed. A home, my family, an education, and opportunity, but something felt like it was missing. I never felt like I fit in anywhere no matter how hard I tried. I knew there was more for me somewhere, and I hoped to find it, so I left my small town after graduating high school.

After graduating college, I took off for Chicago. Once there, I settled into a life. I found a job, made friends, met a man... And once I started, I was unstoppable, continuing down this path – whether it was the right life for me or not.

I was an overachieving perfectionist. I always did well in school and at work, the student and employee who strived for others to tell her "Good job!" If I needed to work eighty hours that week to get the project done, I did it. If they wanted me to travel to three cities in one week across five time zones, I did it. Stay the weekend in Arkansas to save on expenses? Sure, I'll find something to do! (And I realized that Arkansas is actually really pretty).

I made changes. I changed jobs regularly. I moved every year for many years, I divorced my first husband and then my second. I recognize now that all these changes were my inner wisdom telling me "Abort! Abort!" but I kept pushing the messages down and kept pushing through. This is what we're supposed to do, I kept telling myself.

After graduating with my MBA, I was diagnosed with Stage 2 melanoma and then divorced my first husband.

The marriage had long been over, and it was finally time to end it. We had returned from our honeymoon five years prior to voice messages, from which I learned that he was three to six months late on all his bills...credit cards, student loans, car payment. Three years prior, he'd had an affair. When I found out, he apologized and did everything he could to "make up for it" but it wasn't enough. But I was working full time, going to grad school at night, and traveling for work, and my brain couldn't add divorce to the to-do list.

Our marriage hit a breaking point when I had melanoma. I had little mobility and I was hallucinating from the pain, and he chose to spend most evenings out rather than being with or helping me. I hit my breaking point on a Saturday eight days after my surgery, when he decided to spend the day with his friends.

I decided to make sweeping changes and start fresh across various aspects of my life. I'd earned my MBA and found a new job. I was still healing from melanoma but took off on a search to find a new home. I put my birth information on adoption registries to look for my biological family. A friend asked if I was sure that I wanted to blow up my entire life, and I said YES.

Looking back now, you'd think that I would have continued on this path to create a more aligned life, but once again I got caught up in others' expectations and what I should do.

I continued putting my all into my career, married and divorced a new partner, and neglected my own well-being, which led to further health issues.

The signs were all there that this life wasn't working, but I continued to ignore them.

In my forties, I experienced a "very dark period of my life." I had debilitating vertigo, and the medications they prescribed caused epilepsy. My body was betraying me, and no one knew how to help me. I went to various specialists who prescribed various medications. I ramped up on each medication, then ramped off when it didn't help. None of my doctors would help me get off the original medication because it resolved the worst of the vertigo. My body was rebelling against me, and I was miserable.

At the same time, my partner was a heavy drinker. We would break up when he was drinking heavily, then get back together when he was on his best behavior trying to win me back. He passed away during this time from the effects of alcohol on his body.

Sadly, it took almost another decade for me to reinvent my life into something more fulfilling, and the impetus was discovering in 2019 that my name and birthdate had been changed.

I was having an identity crisis, and I didn't know how to fix it.

I was reconciling what I'd learned with the person I'd been and the stories I'd created about who my biological parents were and how I'd come to be.

In 2020, my crisis hit me harder than ever.

I'd started a new position at the beginning of the pandemic, and I realized that I no longer enjoyed my career. The disconnection from loved ones brought on by the pandemic was affecting my mental health, and I wasn't able to have a big celebration for my 50th birthday.

I was in crisis mode, and I began to think "If this is my life, I don't want to live it."

When I left the new job, I took off on a solo road trip to find myself. I didn't know who I was or what I wanted, but I knew that my life couldn't continue on like this.

It took time, self-discovery, soul-searching, and study to realize that we have the power to *shape our own identity* and to learn how to do so.

While my experience of brutally confronting my identity is somewhat unique, it underscored the crucial role that identity plays in our lives and how it can either enable or hinder us in creating the lives we desire.

The first time I heard about "identity," the concept resonated with me. I'd never considered my identity before, but it was there in all the questions I'd been asking myself.

Who am I?
What am I doing here?

And when talking with someone about my struggle with having

two identities and trying to reconcile who I'd always been and what I'd learned, they asked,

> *Why do you have to choose?*
> *Those aren't your only options.*

And I suddenly realized that we *can decide who we want to be.*

The past doesn't define us. We can take our experiences and decide what we want to do and who we want to be next. I didn't have to be Tina or Susan; I could create this next version of myself into whomever pleased me.

With this realization, I went on a quest to discover what I wanted to do, who I wanted to be, and how I wanted to live my life. I experienced the magic of finding my identity in this world and I began living authentically to my desires.

I realized through this journey that I had been living a life that society told me I should want: do well in school, get a good job, get married, buy a house, and have kids. When we retire, then we can travel, and enjoy life and our grandchildren.

The conditioning and pressure begin at a young age and persist well into adulthood. Friends ask when we're getting married and then when we're having children, wanting us all to follow the same path together.

While this life path is the right path for some, it's not right for everyone. Even when it starts as the right path, life changes and we change. Often in midlife, we find ourselves wondering if this is all there is, experiencing a lack of purpose, fulfillment, and joy in how we are living our lives.

To fully understand this transformation, we must first dive into the factors that have significantly influenced our sense of identity.

I want to take you on a journey to explore how societal expectations shape and condition who you are and what you want. We'll examine how your identity is formed and discover how you can reinvent yourself into the person and life you want.

PEELING BACK THE LAYERS OF IDENTITY

Your identity influences every aspect of your life. It consists of various elements that come together to create your unique sense of self, and it can evolve as you go through changes in life. Key influences from childhood that shape your identity include:

- Your family including where and how you were raised, your culture, who you grew up with, the era you grew up in, and the experiences you had
- The people you spent time with in the past or present
- Everything and everyone you were exposed to including religion, school, historical events such as war or economic downturn, significant emotional events, and media and advertising.

Your *identity* is what you *identify* with.

WHAT CAUSES AN IDENTITY SHIFT?

There are many events that can trigger a desire for something different and an identity shift. My experience includes being laid off, divorce, illness, starting over in new cities, changing careers, starting a company, and the deaths of a partner and a three-month-old nephew. Others experience this when becoming an empty nester. It can also be a result of realizing your mortality and questioning if this is how you want to continue to live your life.

One example of an identity shift is when someone gets divorced, going from being a spouse to being a single person. Not only does their identity shift, but the identity of "a single person" is shaped by their perception of what it means to be single. Is being single freeing or depressing? Is the world full of opportunities or bleak if they are single?

Consider any shifts you've experienced in your life and how that has changed your priorities and values.

HOW YOU DESCRIBE YOURSELF IS YOUR IDENTITY

You might associate yourself with your career, achievements, or education. A common question when you meet new people is, "What do you do?" People also connect over where they went to school or their level of education.

It might be what you look like, such as your age or physical features.

You could mention your personal traits such as your personality. "I'm an introvert, extrovert, ISTJ. I have a fiery temper. I'm a good listener."

It could be your passions, hobbies, and interests. "I'm a mountain biker. I enjoy baking bread. I like to paint."

You could talk about your life experiences and challenges you've overcome.

You might mention the roles you play. "I'm a parent, spouse, entrepreneur."

You could discuss your values, beliefs, or spiritual or religious views.

You might talk about the traditions, customs, language, and values of your culture.

These are just a few ways that you might describe who you are—all vital aspects of your identity.

How would you describe your identity and how has it changed over the years?

With radical honesty, you can achieve radical authenticity.

Your magic is hidden in your willingness to be vulnerable and confront your deepest fears and insecurities. With radical honesty, you can achieve radical authenticity, and there is nothing more freeing than that.

YOU CAN TRANSFORM YOUR LIFE BY UNDERSTANDING YOUR SUBCONSCIOUS MIND

95% of our brain operates on autopilot. These are subconscious thoughts that run in the background, and they enable you to do things without consciously thinking about what to do. An example of your subconscious running the show is driving. When you first learned to drive, you had to think about all the steps you needed to take—step on the gas, step on the brake, shift, watch your mirrors. Once you're an experienced driver, your subconscious mind takes over and you don't have to remember to take each action.

When you drive somewhere you often visit and don't remember driving to get there, that's because your mind knows how to drive and how to get to your destination. You may even zone out and wonder how you got there.

Bringing awareness to your thoughts enables you to make more conscious choices. When you take a pause, you can decide if this thought, emotion, belief, or habit is what you want or if you want to choose differently.

YOU CAN CHOOSE YOUR IDENTITY

By consciously choosing what you want in your life, you can cultivate a life that lights you up. This means you consciously consider and choose:

- the thoughts running through your head
- the beliefs you have about yourself, the world, and those around you
- the emotions you feel
- the habits and patterns driving your life.

Are your current thoughts, beliefs, emotions, and habits working *for* you or *against* you?

What would your life be like if you could change them?

REINVENTION DOESN'T HAVE TO BE BIG, HARD, OR SCARY

Even if you wanted to remain the same person, doing the same things, with the same people ten years from now, the world will evolve around you. The people around you will evolve.

You might get laid off, decide to pursue a new career, or start your own company.

If you have kids, they'll be in different places in their lives, which will make your relationship with them different.

You might become a grandparent. How would that change your family relationships and how you spend your time?

You might decide to pursue new hobbies, learn new things, or travel to places you haven't been before.

These are part of your identity and a form of reinvention.

Reinvention can be small, incremental changes made over time, but the most important part is staying open to what lights you up right now, rather than getting stuck in a rut just because that's how you've been living. It's about consciously choosing how you want to live your life and what you do with your time, as it's easy to fall into a routine when you're so busy that you're functioning on autopilot and every day looks the same.

If you could reinvent some aspect of your life, what would you focus on right now? What do you want to be different?

PRIORITIZE YOURSELF

Many women find it difficult to prioritize themselves because they are often busy taking care of others, neglecting their own wants and needs. Eventually, some wake up one day and question who they are, what has happened to their lives, and how they can reclaim what they want moving forward.

I often hear, "I feel like I should have all this figured out by now." These women feel stuck, overwhelmed, and even ashamed that this life they've built for themselves isn't satisfying them. They wonder what's wrong with them because everyone else seems happy with their lives.

It's okay to live your life based on what you want and to want something different than what you have, even if everyone else seems so happy with it—and I want you to know that you are not alone.

Prioritizing yourself to figure out *"What's next for **me**?"* is an act of self-love.

TUNE IN TO YOURSELF AND IGNORE THE OUTSIDE NOISE

The world is filled with so many expectations, and if you're constantly busy, you can easily ignore your internal guidance about what you truly want.

But when you focus on the magic of being your authentic self, peel away the layers of societal expectations, and remove your self-imposed limitations, you can live a blissful life that feels like your greatest adventure.

What if you could design and live a life that feels so blissful and empowered by the unique magic that exists in you?

It's the seemingly unimportant things that hold the most magic.

Seeing a rainbow, watching the hummingbird outside your office window, seeing a deer hop across a field, laughing so hard you cry, or singing and dancing to your favorite song—these moments are truly enchanting.

For years, I ignored these tiny magical moments, always searching for big moments of joy and magic. But once you start to observe the world more closely, you will find that magical moments are everywhere. When you take notice and feel the joy they bring, you will start to see even more.

HOW MAGICAL WOULD IT FEEL TO REINVENT YOURSELF AND YOUR LIFE INTO THE TRUEST, MOST BLISSFUL VERSION OF YOU?

Imagine living a life that feels like an adventure, with each day full of bliss, passion, and joy. Too often, we settle for mediocrity, suppressing our truest desires and simply going through the motions. When we do this, we allow life to happen to us, rather than actively creating the life we want.

Choosing to live reactively will keep you stuck in the same patterns of life you've always known. But what if you could choose differently? What if you could reinvent yourself and your life, aligning with your deepest passions and desires, and experiencing the fullest, most joyful version of yourself?

Are you ready to take charge and create a life that feels like the greatest adventure? The journey to your authentic self awaits, and it promises a life of magic and bliss.

The choice is yours: to live reactively or to step into the enchanting possibility of reinvention.

Are you ready to choose differently and become the truest, most blissful version of yourself?

ABOUT TINA WEFER

Tina Wefer is a Reinvention Catalyst, Founder of The Reinvention Code, and bestselling author of Women Excelling Everywhere. Tina experienced her own identity and midlife crisis after discovering at age 49 that her name and birthdate had been changed. She realized she hated her career and her life, and realized she couldn't continue living the same way. She left her job, took off on a solo road trip, found herself, and learned how to create a blissful, authentic life in the process.

Now, Tina helps women escape mediocre lives, reinvent their identities and their lives, and live lives filled with bliss. She works with women navigating midlife or when starting over, leveraging her personal experience with being laid off, divorce, illness, starting over in a new location, and the deaths of a partner and a three-month-old nephew in her work to help women live their best, most authentic lives.

Website: www.IdentityReinvention.com/resources
Email: mailto:hello@IdentityReinvention.com
Facebook: www.facebook.com/groups/midlifereinventionsociety

11
FOCUS ON THE MAGIC 22-DAY EXPERIENCE

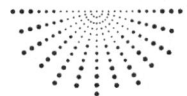

WITH ADRIANA MONIQUE ALVAREZ

DAY 1 - MANIFESTING MAGIC

Your Toolbox Ready?

Before going on a trip, I love packing my suitcase. When I devote myself to a particular focus, I gather my tools. So, for today let's do this...

What are 3-12 things you can deliberately focus on and appreciate?

These are where you will turn your attention when the brain wants to rehash why your mother-in-law is a Jackhole Jackie.

It's where you will go when you wake up irritated with a migraine.

It's what you'll hyper-focus on when your mind wanders to all things you don't yet have or all the ways things aren't happening how or when you want them to. If chemicals, hormones, emotions, thoughts, beliefs, and words attempt to hijack this whole manifesting your biggest dreams thing, you want to have a plan.

I recommend writing your 3-12 things down on a piece of paper or in the notes on your phone.

Here's mine...

I am deliberately focusing on and appreciating:

- Spring flowers and blooming trees
- Kittens
- Warmer weather and longer days
- Baseball season
- Pineapple
- Fennel cardamom coriander tea
- Fresh juices
- Yin yoga
- Durga chanting music
- Walks
- Sunsets
- 6-4-6 deep breathing
- Writing and blogging
- Rescue Remedy
- Rose hair and face oil
- Face massages
- Fresh ginger water
- The smell of burning incense
- Dancing to 90's music
- Driving through the car wash
- Laying on the ground

Go get your list and toolbox ready.

We are more than chemicals, hormones, emotions, thoughts, beliefs, and words.
We are more than our experiences and circumstances.
We are eternal.
We are powerful.
We are divine.

And in this 22-day experience, we choose to remember and act like it.

DAY 2

Repeat After Me or maybe even write it down and put it on your fridge...

I am open to receiving everything the Universe has for me.
I am loved and supported beyond my comprehension.
All is well.
It is safe for me to enjoy my life.
It is safe for me to enjoy my day.

DAY 3

A state of gratitude sends out a signal that you are ready to receive more. What are you in deep gratitude for? This might be the perfect thing to write in a journal or to discuss over dinner.

We have water running around the property and the ponds are filling up. Everything is green and blooming. We will have lots of fruit this summer. My family is healthy, and we know how to heal ourselves. We have friends who come to baseball games, give us steaks, make us pretzels, and come over for breakfast.

What about you?

DAY 4

Relationships are incredibly important to our overall well-being. Who are the people who love and accept you exactly as you are? Who are the ones who walked through dark times with you? Who celebrates with you? Who do you do all the above for? Let's pause and notice.

A handwritten card or text to your people thanking them for being there would feel good to everybody.

Look at who you get to do life with in all the various seasons.

DAY 5

Rest. Replenish. And know it's inevitable. You are blooming. What's yours cannot miss you.

Take incredible care of yourself. How does that look for you? Consider what one or two things you do for yourself on a regular basis. That might be getting to bed at a certain time, eating real food, getting out in nature, calling the people who matter to you, noticing and acknowledging how good you are doing.

What does taking impeccable care of yourself look like today?

DAY 6

What are you withholding from yourself UNTIL?

I will be happy with myself when...
I can relax when...

FOCUS ON THE MAGIC 22-DAY EXPERIENCE

I will do this after this....

Joy, excitement, pleasure, and optimism are things we can grant ourselves today no matter what.

Most people feel more comfortable with pain than pleasure. Most people are chemically addicted to stress and create it for themselves. You aren't most people.

How good can you feel, just because?
And for how long can you bask in it?

That's what you are experimenting with in this experience. What might transpire inside of you if you felt good every day for twenty-two days?

DAY 7

What to do when you feel the spectrum of emotions or when you feel bad? Feel it. Acknowledge it. Let it be with you. And then you get to decide how long you want to do so.

We can feel sadness, grief, anger, rage, disappointment, and discouragement WITHOUT making it the focus of the day, week, or lifetime. I learned this when I had a full-term stillbirth.

I could let the range of emotions move through me and I noticed it didn't serve me to dedicate my life to them. It is incredibly exhausting to focus my attention, more often than not, on things I do not like or on things that do not feel good. It's energizing when I choose to highlight and amplify the good in myself, others, and the world. So, I don't pretend. I feel what I feel.

FOCUS ON THE MAGIC

And I feel so much better when I decide where my focus will be.

What are you paying more attention to? How easy can you let it be?

DAY 8

The power of breathing. In the spring of 2022 my friend and client Nicolette, who lives in Grand Junction called me and invited me to go to a Joe Dispenza event with her in Denver. I was finishing writing my one-woman show and was set to perform it a couple of months later. We had a dozen book launches on the calendar. It wasn't an ideal time for me to go, but I felt in my gut like it was the ideal thing, so I said yes and flew to Denver. I had read his books and listened along to his meditations for years but that didn't prepare me for what I walked into...

3000 people in a room! For the first two days, he taught a lot and then on the last day, he said, "We are going to do this. We are going to breathe until we get your head and your heart on the same page and then every cell in your body will respond and harmonize." I have done yoga and meditation for decades. I thought I knew how to breathe, but I had never gone as far as he took us. All 3000 of us were in our chairs, feet on the floor, sitting up tall and we followed his instructions on various lengths of inhalations and exhalations.

About the time my brain was saying...

How long are we going to do this, he mentions we are going to do it for hours.
Hours!

The guy is radical. Intense. Possibly insane—that's what I thought right then. After my mind stopped arguing it slipped into a euphoria I had never experienced before. My senses were heightened in a good way.

I could feel just how good I felt. Every cell in my body felt good. My mind was no longer churning its old thoughts. My heart wasn't aching. For the first time since 2018 when Nina went into that Albanian soil, I wasn't in pain. I wasn't grieving. And friend Nicolette, the sweetest friend, she wasn't reeling from the painful divorce that broke her heart just a year earlier.
Later I learned most of the room had a devastating diagnosis or incurable disease. They go for that session and many experience spontaneous healing and remission.

I thought I knew what breathing was. I thought I had felt the relief it brings. That day I knew it on a deeper level. When I'm on my edge and in the times I have felt lost or like giving up my dad will tell me to breathe. And it always reminds me of the day in that hotel ballroom where I dedicated an entire day to it. You might not spend today doing deep breathing, but as you read this maybe you take the deepest breath you've had today and you remember no matter what is ailing you, your body and mind and every cell inside of you is perfect in every way.

You have access to harmony.
You have access to joy.
And to wholeness.
You are loved!

DAY 9

What are the less celebrated parts of you? The other night I was sitting with two amazing women and the conversation took me back to a moment deep in Mexico. As usual, I had networked myself into a circle with big ideas...

We were going to purchase 1000 acres in the Yucatán, build homes, have a community garden, and a wild school for our kids. I was sent as the scout to look at the property. I was told it had two cenotes. Mayans might have used them for sacrifices, but they now make great swimming holes. It was hot as hell, in fact, this place was way hotter than Kenya or Tucson! I figured I should really get the scoop, so I jumped in! It was beautiful, clean and cool. As I crawled out, the Mexican Realtor with me yelled, "What are you doing?! There are crocodiles in there!"

I smiled and replied...

Good thing I just jumped in! He didn't know if I was brave or crazy. The deal fell through during the 2020 panic. Yesterday a friend sent me a silly reel of the top ten Zodiac signs to wrestle an alligator and win. Wouldn't you know Sagittarius was number two, only beaten out by Aries?

I am not only crazy,
But I am not a finisher,
Quite happy to quit when I am done.
I eat dessert first.
I have zero ability for delayed gratification.
I cannot do work I hate.
And I would much rather be homeless than have a boss.
I am unwilling to be miserable.
I have to have fun every day.
No boring people allowed.
I make it all an adventure.

Most of these traits are not positive ones. Not what we hope to teach kids in school, but I will tell you they are the best parts of me.

What about you? What are the less celebrated parts of you?

DAY 10

The Highlight Reel...

As the dreaded holiday approached I could feel the sting of awareness. The daughter who was not ever going to be here to celebrate Mother's Day with me. The mother who chose to oppose me until I rose up with my sword and cut the cord of connection with her. It had been a day of swirling emotions, and I remembered the highlight reel. It's where I scroll through my day mentally, find the best bits, and string them together to form the day's highlight reel. I fall asleep replaying it over and over.

At the top of the list was the hummingbird. The first one of the season to show up and dance in the window behind Derek's head at breakfast. Hummingbirds remind me of my Grandma Ruth and this was definitely her spirit. She left hummingbirds all over her house for me to find and I keep two in the kitchen and dining room. They are the reminder to find joy in it all. Then I thought of the happy moment of visiting a friend in the afternoon. The breakthrough a dear friend and client in Australia had. The illuminating conversation Derek and I shared and his unwavering presence in my life through every season.

Hugs from the boys.
Food delivered by my dad.
The perfect cup of lavender lemon balm tea.
Work on a local project.

FOCUS ON THE MAGIC

As I added that last one to my highlight reel my eyes watered. Seven months ago, I didn't have this one, and oh how I longed for it. What am I doing here?

Last year I sensed my purpose was to gather people, feed them, and connect them. When I did this through a physical location and local business it was not celebrated. My mom's words started echoing through my head. No one here cares about that. You're spending too much time talking to people. Get to work. Little did she know, that was THE work.

When I got quiet I heard...

Monique, you are here for the land.

What does that mean?
You are here for the land. You are here to love the land and its people.

How do I do that?
Lay on the ground. Lay here until you feel it. Then get up and fill your house with love. Gather people around your table and feed them.

What then?
Do this until further notice.

How will I pay for my life?
Do this until further notice.

Will this replace my publishing company?
Do this until further notice.

I spent the last seven months doing just that. It was a concoction of emotions from bliss and peace to the unsettling feeling only the void commands. The unknown. I could be in the moment, but I couldn't connect any dots.

And as I put together my highlight reel I realized, I had been the seed, the promise and potential, all winter long. Pushed deep in that dark soil by the one whose role in this life has been to oppose me. To test me. To taunt me. To deny me. To doubt me. To push me to the point where I have but two choices…

To be nothing or to be everything I came here to be.

To rise up with the power that only a seed in the soil knows. To push up through that cold, hard dirt to find the light and warmth of the sun. And to be like the irises my Grandma Ruth planted so many years ago…on the verge of blooming.

All my petals are still hidden, but soon they will unfurl. The message that was repeated hundreds, if not thousands of times, Love this land and its people. Lay on the ground until you feel it. Fill your house with love. Gather them around your table and feed them. I did it until I wasn't seeking a solution or trying to solve a riddle. I did it until my own heart healed and I desired nothing more than to be on the land with its people. And wouldn't you know it, around that same table my next steps dropped into my heart out of the big blue sky.

As I built the highlight reel for one day, I felt it all, but most of all liberation.

No one and no thing could possibly thwart me. Only I can do that. No circumstances or curves in the road can throw me off my path. It is written. And certainly, no holiday can rob me of the absolute and perfect joy of being alive…even without a daughter or mother by my side.

I am by my side. And all those people who gather around my table are too.

My trusted highlight reel. I can always count it on to be the place where my heart expands.

Do you do highlight reels at night? What if you re-lived all the best moments of your day as you drifted off to sleep?

DAY 11

When in doubt, look up. That is where our help comes from.
When we raise your head, whether it's to…
Bask in the sun,
Watch the clouds float by,
Count the stars,
Or look for a rainbow…
Our brain and heart shift.
And we remember we are part of the mystery and the cosmos.

What's your way of looking up?

DAY 12

Beauty—every thing has it. The key is slowing down long enough to see it.

What beauty are you noticing today? This could be a beautiful journaling exercise or a question to ask a friend over tea.

DAY 13

It's been said that there are four tiers of conversation:

1. Talking about people.
2. Talking about what you did.
3. Talking about future dreams.
4. Talking about implementing something today that creates the future you want.

One and two keep us in our comfort zones. Three and four move us out of what has been into something new. Whether we have these conversations with one or two or a group doesn't matter, as long as we have them. Words are the wand, and we are the Magician.

Who do you have dynamic conversations with and how often do they happen?

DAY 14

This month is all about connecting to what feels good. The stuff that reminds us that we are safe and loved and that have access to a loving and benevolent Universe. Next month we can complain and be lemon suckers. ;)

A friend recently sent me a photo and I realized how much I owe that brave sixteen-year-old.
My life today is the way it is largely because she didn't bend. She didn't follow the path and she didn't please others nearly as much as she pleased herself.

She broke off an engagement,
Decided against college,

And left the country.
She didn't focus on getting married or on a career.
She followed the adventure inside of her.
And she trusted herself even when she wasn't sure it would work out.

At some point, she realized life isn't about how smart you are or how rich you are, but it's more about how bold and brave we are willing to be. The audacity to be herself. That's the gold.

What about you?
Do you recall those times you were brave and bold and so ridiculously you?
What age do you look back at and celebrate?

DAY 15

We know we can handle stress, trauma, and sleepless nights. Can we handle joy?

Derek is our family DJ. He puts together playlists of music and one of them is titled BASEBALL.

On our way to games, we turn it up and sing along. Last night we kicked it off with Let's Get Loud by Jennifer Lopez. I smile when the boys really belt it out. By the time we arrive at the game it doesn't matter what happens next, we already won.

Do you love music?
How do you use it to shift what you're feeling?

DAY 16

Scatter Something...

What's the resource you feel the most scarcity around?

Time
Money
Relationships
Knowledge
Confidence
Happiness

How can you scatter that today? For example, with money, take a few coins from your car or junk drawer and leave them where they will be found by others. Take the thing you desire more of and in a small way gift it to others. Talk about a good feeling! Woo!

DAY 17

Get Fucking Unreasonable!

What most people aren't ready to look at is their level of living is directly related to their level of insanity. Most people are reasonable. AKA boring and forgettable. Rarely getting what they desire. Existing, but barely.

They are afraid to be full-tilt themselves.
They are afraid of criticism.
They are afraid of getting canceled.
They need people to like and accept them.
They need a sale.
They need a nod.

They need approval.
They need confirmation.
They need so much they cannot be unreasonable.

What does this look like?

Standards.
Setting standards.
Across the board.
This is how it works in this world that I created.

Leaders.
Revolutionaries.
Are unreasonable.
Always have been!

People look at their vision, their passion, and their ideas and think to themselves, "They are bonkers!"

Damn straight. You cannot leave a lasting imprint without at least a touch of insanity. And once you get there, make sure you are particular about staying in close proximity to the other wild ones.

The tame ones will talk about you.
The ones who envy you will criticize you.
They will mock you.
They will attempt to undermine you.
They will ignore you and leave you out.

But they only have as much power as you give them.

Stop giving them your ear.
Stop making space for them at your table.
Stop longing for what they can never offer you.

Start turning it up. Go bigger. Get more unreasonable. Gather those who get it. And there are ALWAYS those who get you. You came here to be the most YOU you can be. And that requires guts! It's the way to living out this adventure fully.

Where are you SO freaking tired of being reasonable and realistic?

DAY 18

Rose-Colored Glasses

It's easy to notice what is lacking, and what can be improved. It's easy to spot where people's shortcomings are. It's easy to nag. To complain. To talk about what is off. To take people for granted. To miss the magic in the mundane.

And Yet...

When we can put those rose-colored glasses on, even for just a day. When we commit to seeing the best in people. To noticing how much they care. To their gifts and strengths. To their smile and heart.

When we verbalize what we appreciate. When we show them what they mean to us. When we find ways to pause and connect. With a stranger or the person closest to us, we are different.

Love floods us. Feel good chemicals wash over our brain and then awe returns. Life is so different when it's viewed through rose-colored glasses, even if it's just for a day.

What if one day a week there was no room for complaining or criticism, but instead a dedication to only seeing the best in everyone and everything? One day a month?

What might shift individually and collectively?

DAY 19

Releasing It

All it takes is a few still moments to notice...

The emotions that aren't yours. The moments that didn't go as planned. The flops and failures. Guilt, shame and fear. The weight of unmet expectations. Disappointing, frustrating experiences. Hurt and pain inflicted and initiated. The fragmented you. What's dead and done.

And today we can release it.
We can write about it.
Talk about it.
Pray about it.
Or send it down into the earth to be recycled.
But it can leave our mind and body.
Watching it, breathing it, shaking it, crying it...OUT.

Part of feeling good is knowing when to lay it down.
What is too heavy to keep carrying?

DAY 20

Pick Your Pocket...

As you think about your day and what's on the schedule, can you find a pocket of time for something that nurtures you?

It might be:

The perfect cup of tea.
Taking a bath.
Laying with your legs up the wall.
Going for a walk.
Taking a nap.
A few minutes of journaling.
A rampage of appreciation.
Watching the sunset.
Pulling a card.
A homemade meal.
Meditation.
Prayer.
Creating a highlight reel.

Pick your pocket once a day and notice how much it affects your life. What's your pocket going to be today?

DAY 21

Find the Funny & Mine the Absurd...

Interesting things happen when you become "internet famous." When posts go viral and big names put you on their podcasts and publications put you in their magazines. I love people watching and the internet is people watching on steroids! Human nature is fascinating to me. To watch how people react and respond. What pushes their buttons? What makes them laugh and what makes them cry?

By 2018 I was starting to receive more and more private messages—that's haters' and critics' favorite place to communicate about everything I did. How I raised my kids outside the US, because God knows it's unsafe to raise kids anywhere else. How I posted or went live every day, because God knows that's not allowed by people too terrified to be seen or heard. How I spent my money, because God knows a woman who has money is the most selfish of all.

But their favorite topics seemed to be...

How my marriage wasn't real, and Derek was a figment of my imagination or better yet a horrible person, because God knows good relationships don't exist and the family concept is so dead.

How I had a full-term stillbirth because I was a bad person, a horrible mother, or had done something awful in a past life.

How I should use my influence for more than making money, talking about taboo topics, being funny and sarcastic. And how I should stop talking about lemon suckers and leave Jackhole Jackie alone.

I'm talking about 75-100 people a day advising and educating me on how I should...

Raise my kids.
Live my life.
Market my business.
Spend my money.
Be married.
Grieve my daughter.
Communicate and express myself.

The irony wasn't lost on me. I had grown one of the largest publishing companies in the world by doing what I did. I championed women to tell their stories and be fully self-expressed.

And the curse of success was this...

What I fought for them to have, they didn't believe I deserved for myself.

Fascinating.
Don't do that.
Don't talk that way.
Don't be free.
Don't be yourself.
Be who WE want you to be.
Not a chance in hell!

One day I was talking to my friend Terrie about the latest message: a lady in Australia who would clear my bad karma and guarantee I would get pregnant again and have a healthy baby for only $100,000. People are fascinating, right!?

She asked me...

Monique, why don't you start writing 8-minute stories about these absurd messages people send you? I started crying. I don't want to! I don't want to give them more space in my day. I had discovered in 2019 that the best thing to do was ignore people and their absurdity. Zero words. Zero attention. No reply. Ever. What was I going to do, dedicate a day to justifying myself and my choices to strangers on the internet? Nope!

Terrie pushed. Seriously, it's the perfect therapy and they are providing you with free content to write and speak about.

Monique, you have to find the funny and mine the absurd!

I agreed to write a story about the lady in Australia. I performed it online to a big audience and afterward, I was HIGH. I felt so good. So FREE! It was another social media sensation and that day I received hundreds of messages saying, "That was amazing!" Writing has truly become not only my therapy, but my favorite addiction, my life raft, and my freedom.

I process life,
People,
Experiences,
And it becomes the contribution.
My offering to you.
A permission slip.
A mantra.
And a battle cry.

I will not change who I am—for anybody.
I will not change the way I communicate.
I will not change the way I do business.
I will not change my views on family.
I will not stop valuing marriage.

But I will be happy to cheer you on to be as you as you can be.

I will never tell you to shut down your voice.
I will never be mad if you make money.
I will never be realistic about your dreams.
I will never define success for you.

How can you find the funny and mine the absurd today?
How can you find a way to laugh?
Life provides us with plenty to work with, what will you do with it?

DAY 22

Celebrate Everything!

When Derek and I met in 2006 in Tucson, Arizona he became the person I trusted to give me feedback about who I am. Not as in, I don't like who you are, be someone different.

As in, do you realize how generous you are and that these people are taking advantage of you? I had been living and traveling solo for a while, so it was interesting to be in this new country and arrangement. One of the things I did often was celebrate. I went networking and met someone amazing—let's go celebrate! I got a new client—let's celebrate! We met three months ago—let's celebrate! When I found a penny on the ground—I celebrated BIG!

I wove this concept of celebration into the work I did. I would ask my clients to make a list of what they were celebrating at the end of each week and month. A few years later I started asking private clients to do it DAILY. Sometimes it started off as a simple acknowledgment of what they completed or focused on in their day.

What I quickly learned is that most people end the day, week, or month by obsessing over what DIDN'T get done, what didn't happen, what didn't go well, and the complete list of what they felt behind on.

That's when I discovered what leads to becoming a...

LEMON SUCKER

Even when really good things happened I couldn't get clients to go to dinner and celebrate it.

That's when I realized celebration is not part of our culture. It's not something we learn at home. Or school or church. Some clients never did give up the almighty lemon, but some did, and the act of celebrating completely transformed their business and life and many times their marriage and family.

This week we are celebrating BIG. It's the last week of school and I built in a half dozen special celebrations. My boys will learn this now and this belief will be deep inside of them because life is definitely worth celebrating!

What are you celebrating today? What celebrations will become standard for you going forward?

ABOUT AMA PUBLISHING

AMA Publishing is an international, award winning publishing company that champions the stories of entrepreneurs who are trailblazers, innovators, and instigators.

Forbes has said that, *"AMA Publishing is helping women reshape the future of publishing."*

We would love to help you tell your story. We have helped thousands of people become international, bestselling authors through our courses, multi-author books, and as solo authors.

Your story, it's ready to be told.

Website: www.amapublishing.co

Made in the USA
Coppell, TX
01 July 2024

34164311R00069